GOLF

HUMOR
By
Charles Hellman and Robert Tiritilli

I0190045

Copyright 2019

LuckySports TM

ALL RIGHT RESERVED
78-218 Silverleaf Ctr.
Palm Desert, CA 92211
www.LuckySportsHumor.com

All rights reserved. Do not duplicate or redistribute in any form. All contents of this book including the concept, elements of design and layout, graphic images and elements, unless otherwise noted, is copyrighted material and protected by trade and other laws and may not be copied or imitated in whole or in part. Violators will be prosecuted to the maximum extent possible. No logo, graphic, character or caption from any page may be copied or retransmitted unless expressly permitted in writing by LuckySports$_{TM}$. Any rights not expressly granted herein are reserved.

ISBN 9780935938579
Illustrations by Robert A. Tiritilli
Cover & Interior Design by Charles S. Hellman
Edited by Charles S. Hellman

Golf Humor Review

There is a point in the life of a golfer when cartoons based on word-play and images that are hysterically funny. This golf humor book is for those who are at that joyous stage in life.

Golf is a club-and-ball sport in which players use various clubs to hit balls into a series of holes on a course in as few strokes as possible. Perhaps no sport has more words, terms, and phrases that lend themselves to humorous reinterpretation based on their literal meaning than golf. The modern game of golf originated in 15th century Scotland. The 18-hole round was created at the Old Course at St Andrews in 1764.

Charles S. Hellman and Robert A. Tiritilli have kept their ability to look at the world through open eyes, and we are the beneficiaries of their vision. You will feel many years younger as you recall the last time you saw the humor in "grownups" taking a sport too seriously.

The book contains over 100 one-paneled, pen and ink drawings reproduced in black and white except on the front and back cover of this soft cover book.

The front cover captures one of the better cartoons and gives you a sense of this book is at its best when it shifts the meaning of a golf phrase into another one. But still within a golf context. Play on words or images gives humor double meaning — the double whammy effect.

These cartoons will tickle your funny bone. Novices, however, will have a few of the cartoons explained to them, as employing golf terms they may not know such as "a Snowman." From the novice's point of view, this will be a four-star book because it doesn't have color inside.

If you are knowledgeable to figure out the "20th hole" cartoon without explanation, this book could be a good gift.

...FORE!!

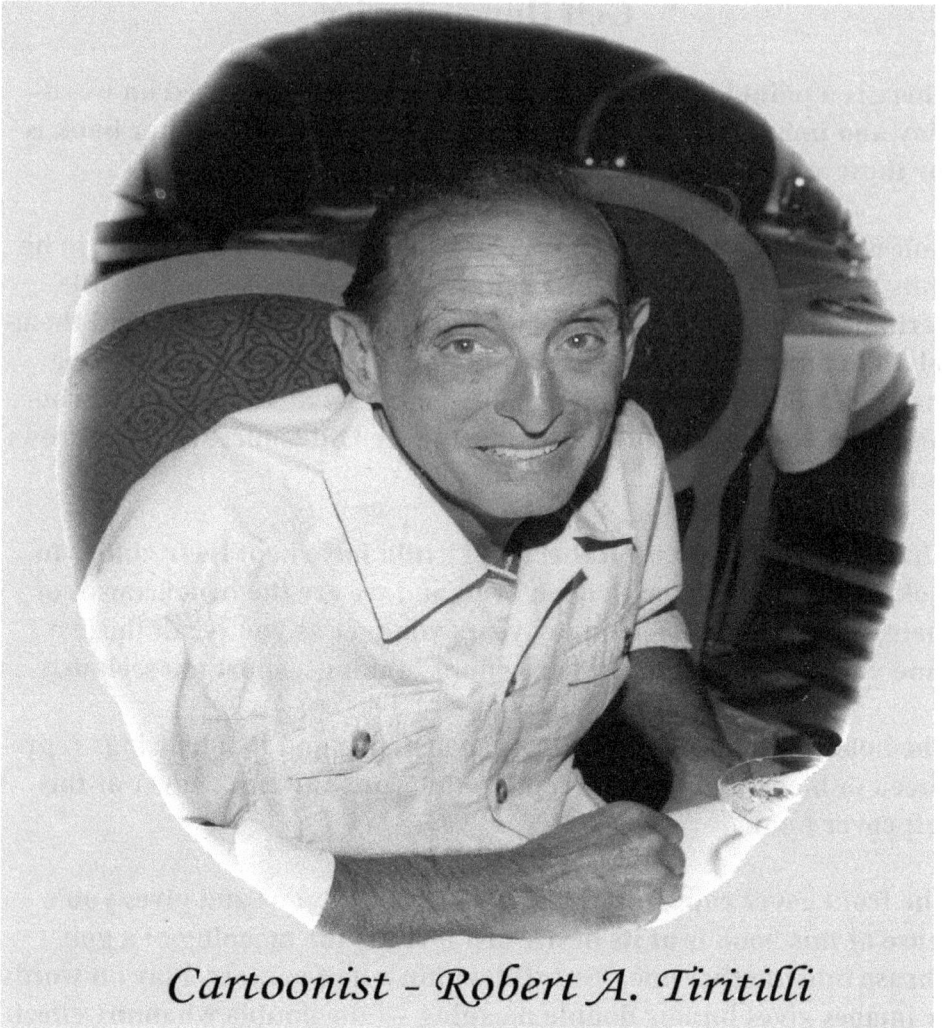

Cartoonist - Robert A. Tiritilli

With years of strong draftsman skills, Robert Tiritilli helped create his outlandish style and talent of sports cartooning by dually employing representative portraiture, and cartoonish lightheartedness.

"I can't believe I gave up smoking, drinking and sex for this!"

5

The last hole of the evening

"Starter... please!"

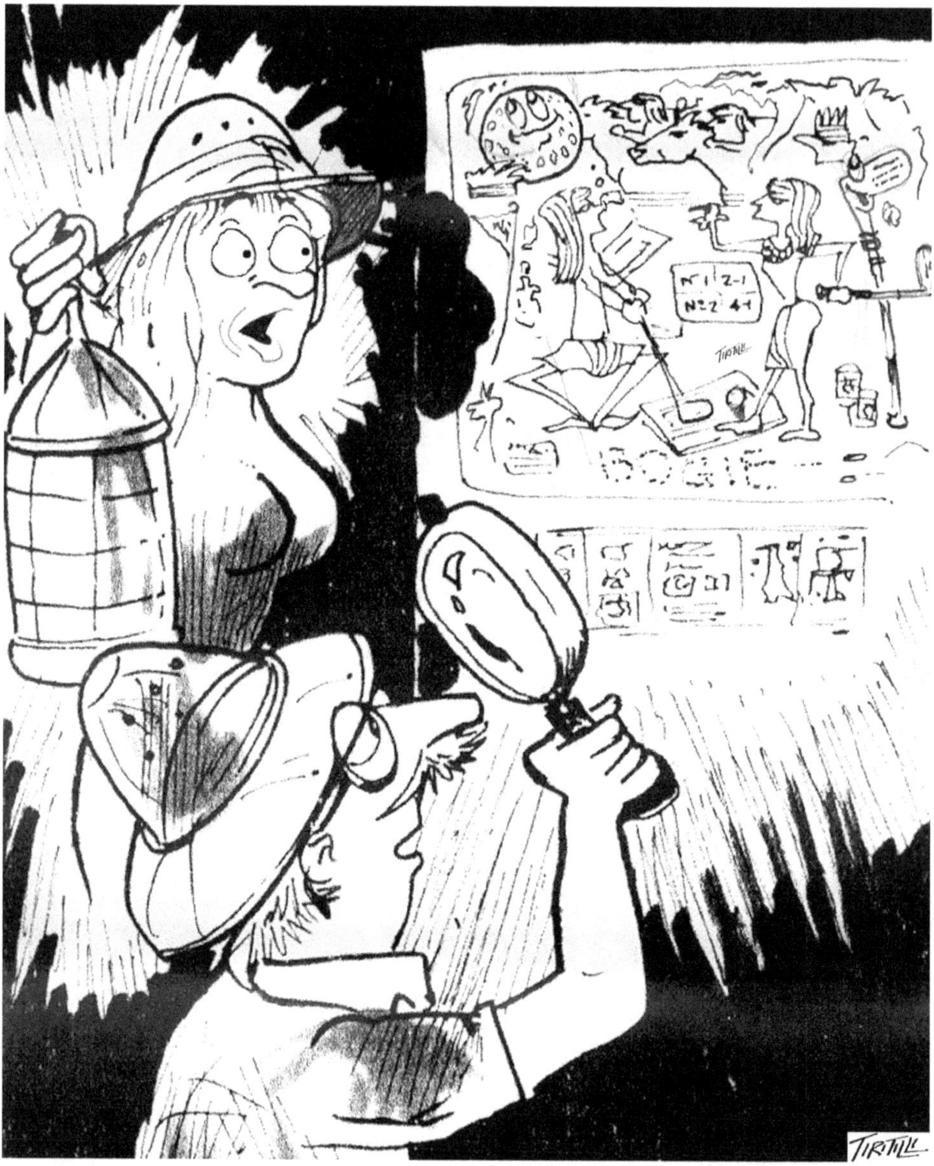

"They're playing... GOLF?"

Tee Time

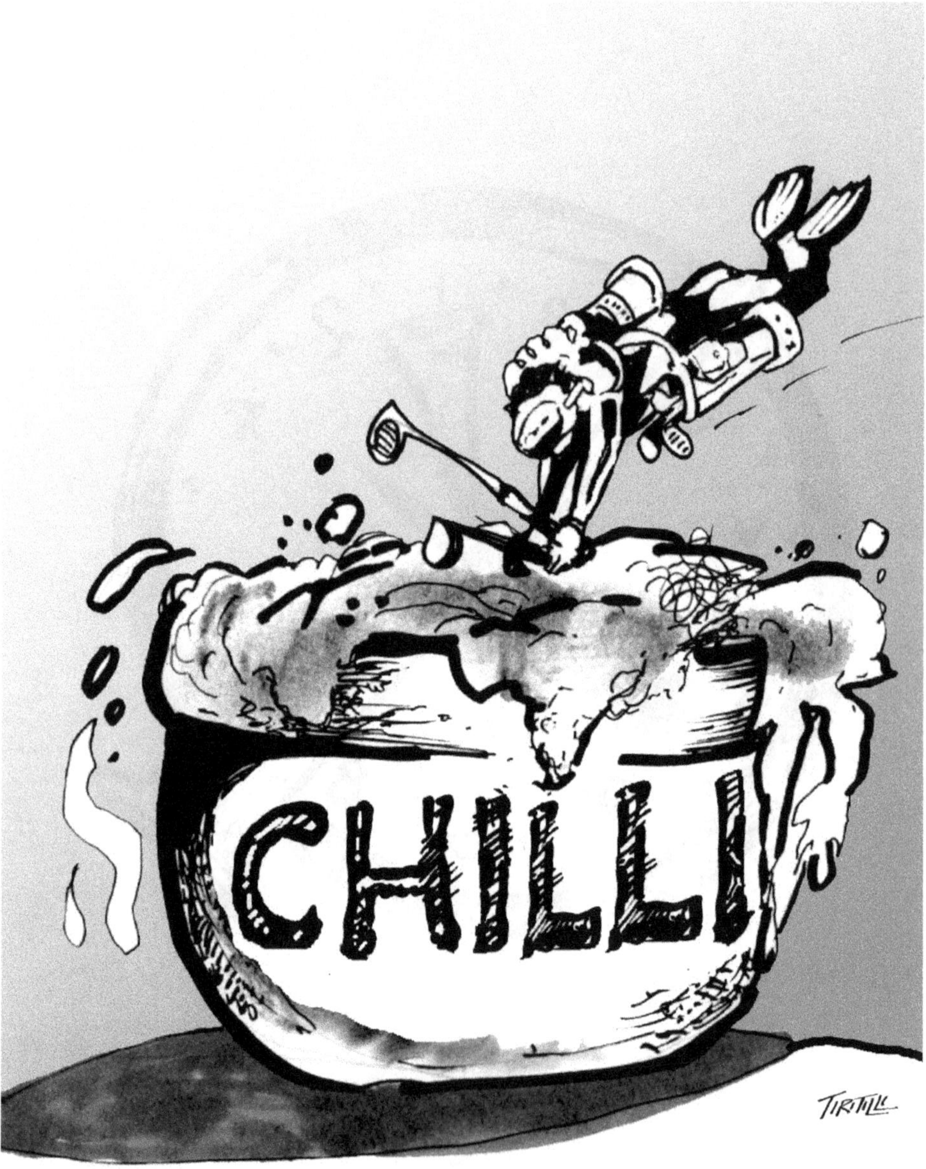
CHILLI
TIRITILLI

Chilli Dip

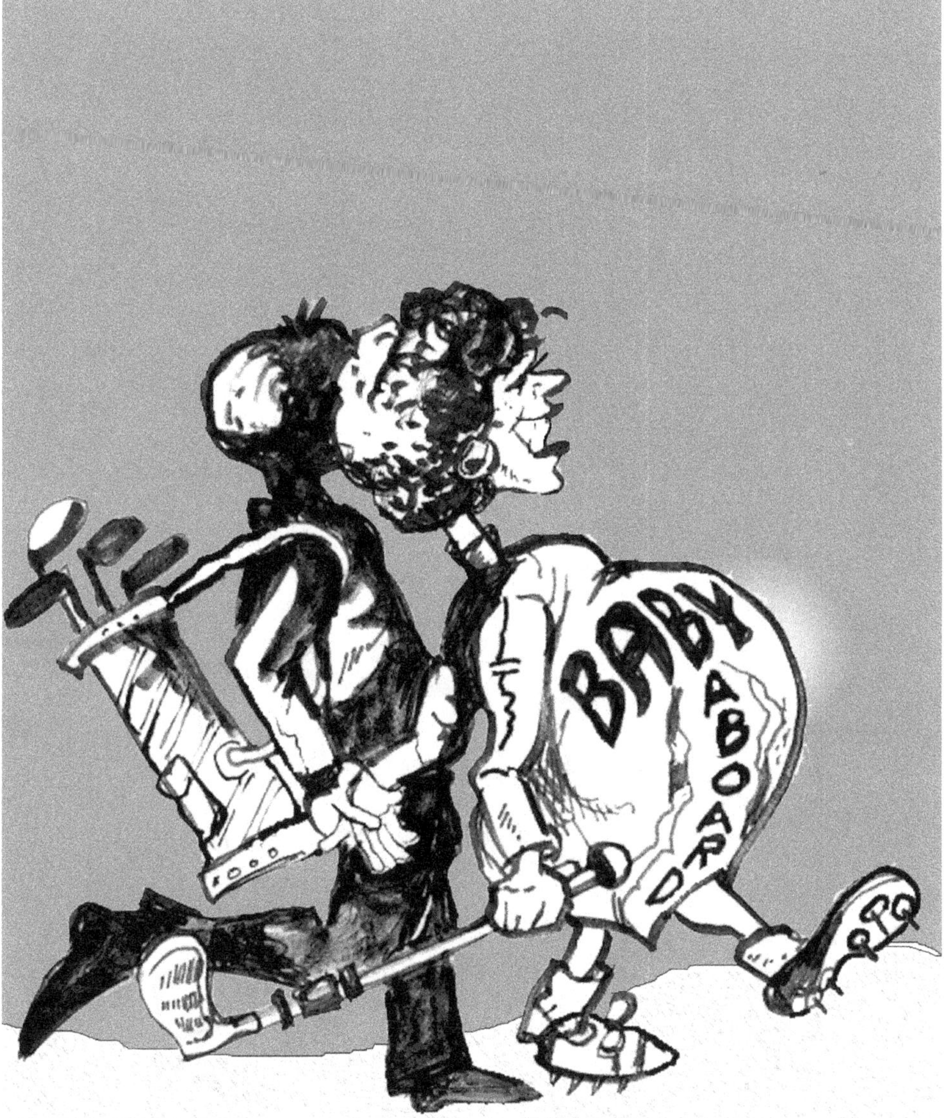
BABY
ABOARD
TIRITILLI

Shotgun Start

"I'm blonde and
I'll swing my way!"

"The owner is a golf course architect."

"My golf game is so bad...
I had my ball retriever regripped!"

"Yes, this is considered to be a hazard."

"The pencil is my favorite club."

16

"I love these golf outings!"

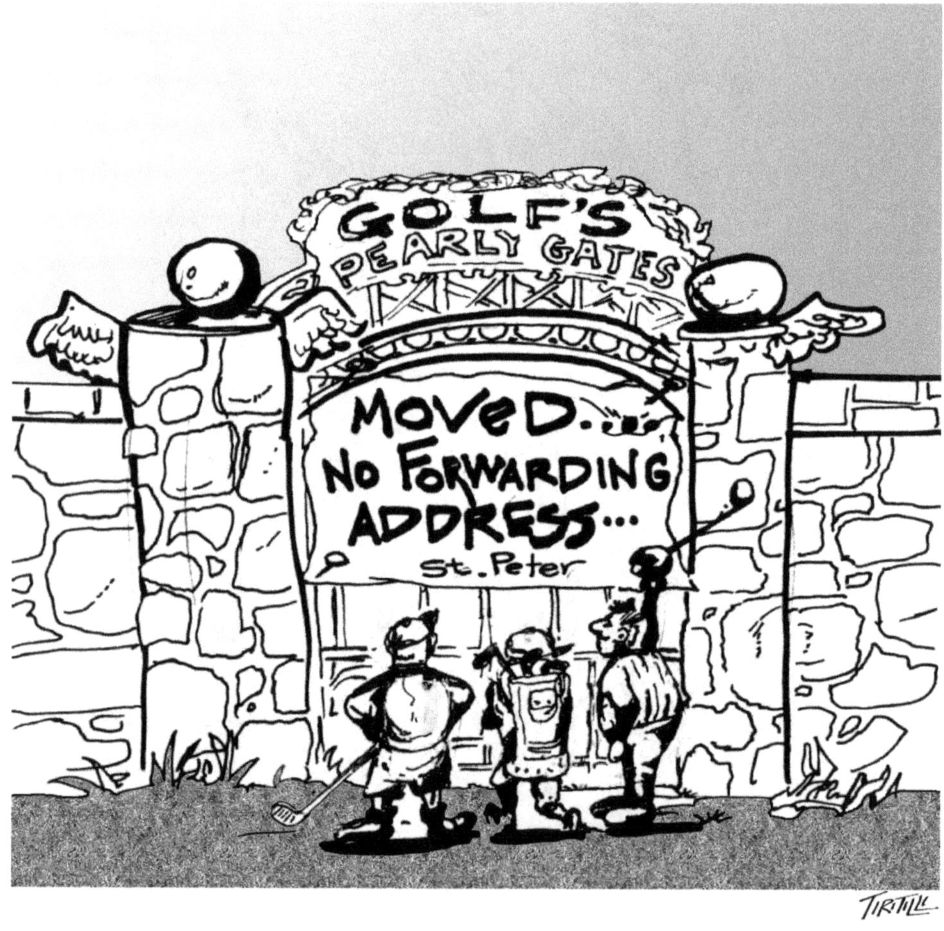
GOLF'S
PEARLY GATES
MOVED...
NO FORWARDING
ADDRESS...
St. Peter
TIRITILLI

Evolution

"When does the 9 o'clock shotgun start?"

"Do a chore and
you'll get back a club."

"You might want to try
a smaller mallet-headed putter."

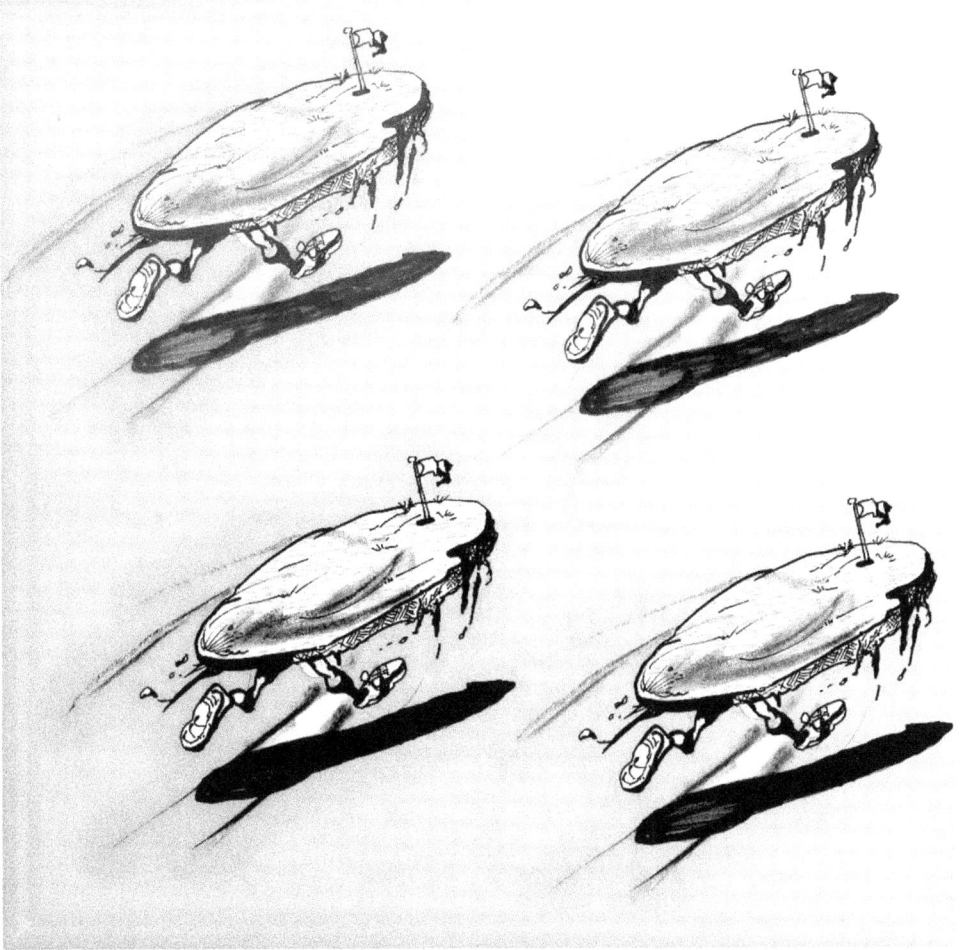

Fast Greens

"Those BELLY putters
can be quite painful."

"The card says... hope your golf score
will be lower than your bowling score."

Long Ball Hitter

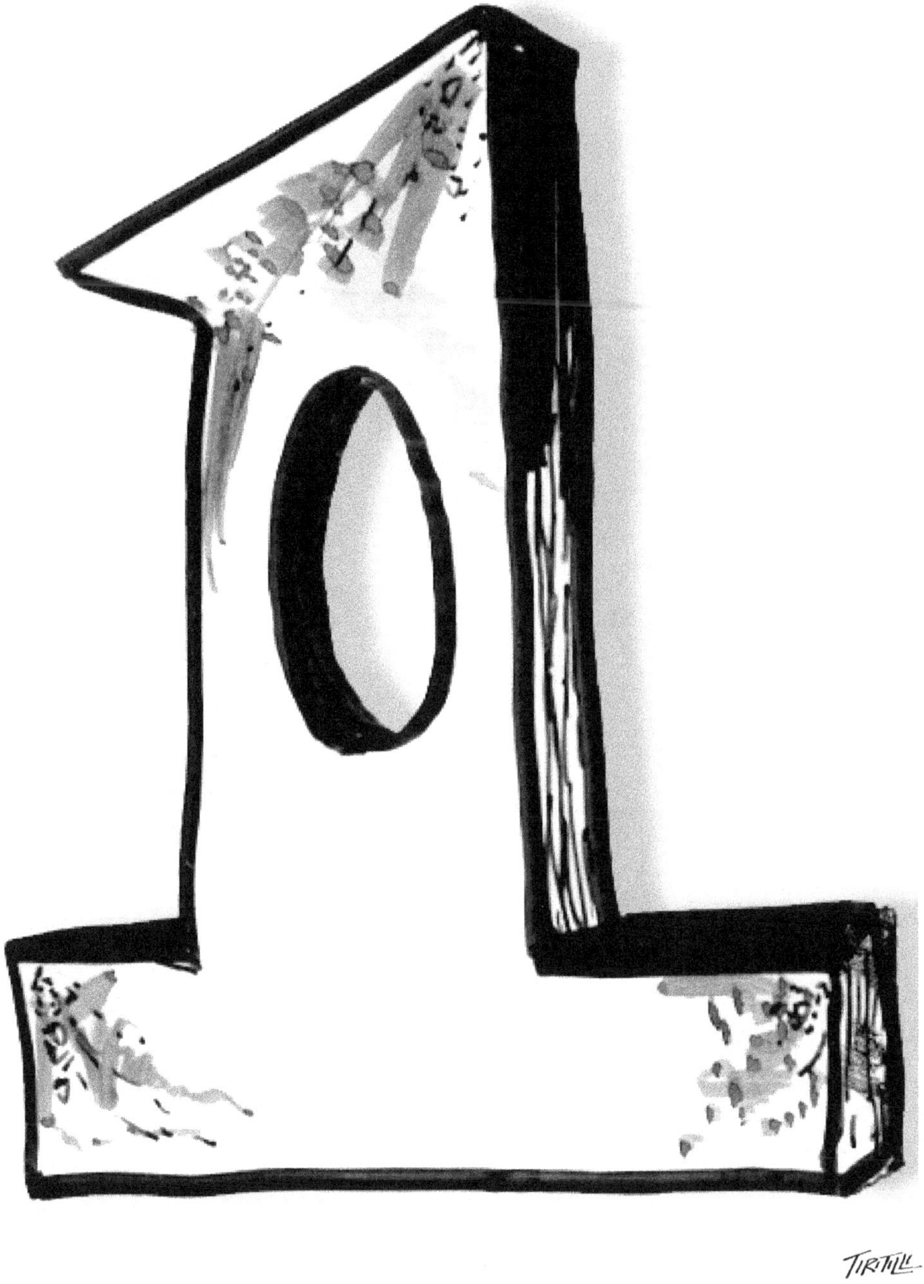
TIRITILLI

Hole-in-one

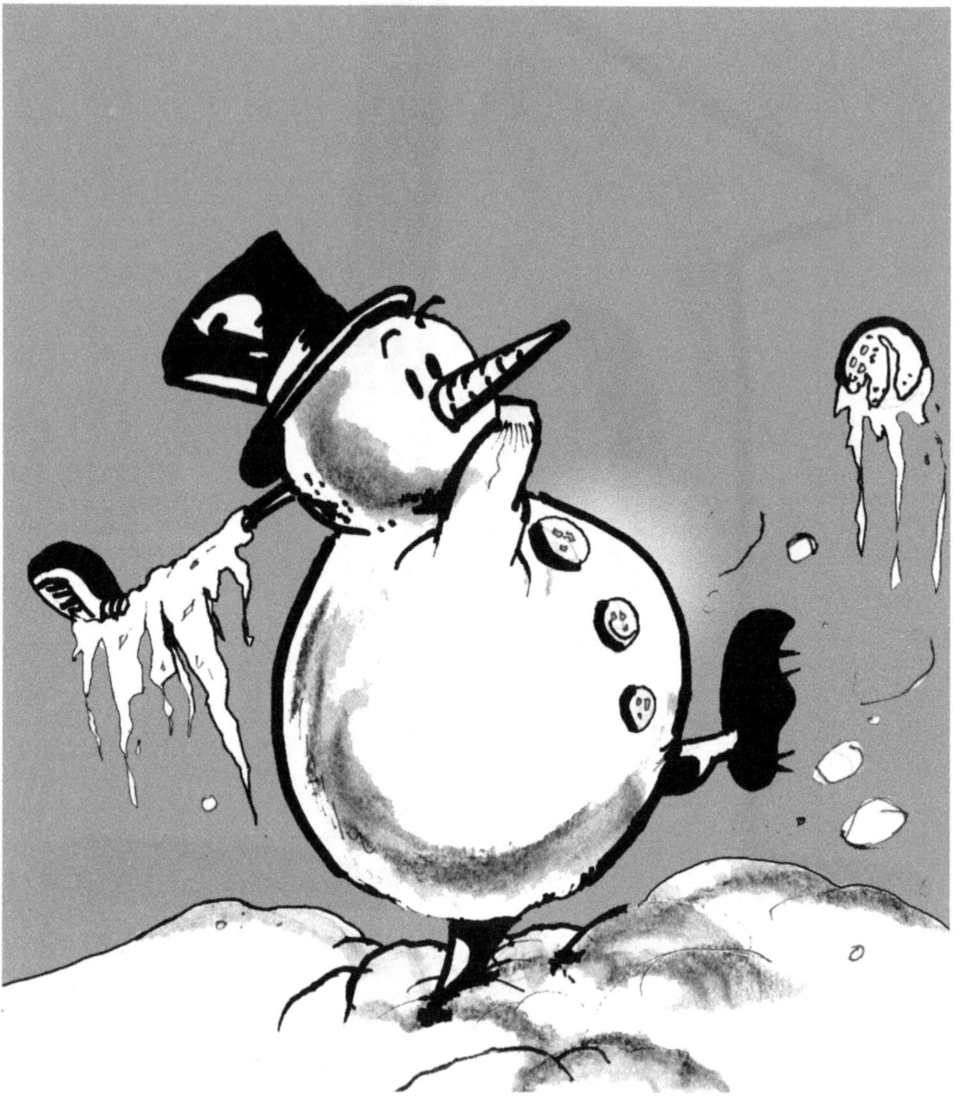

Golfers' 8

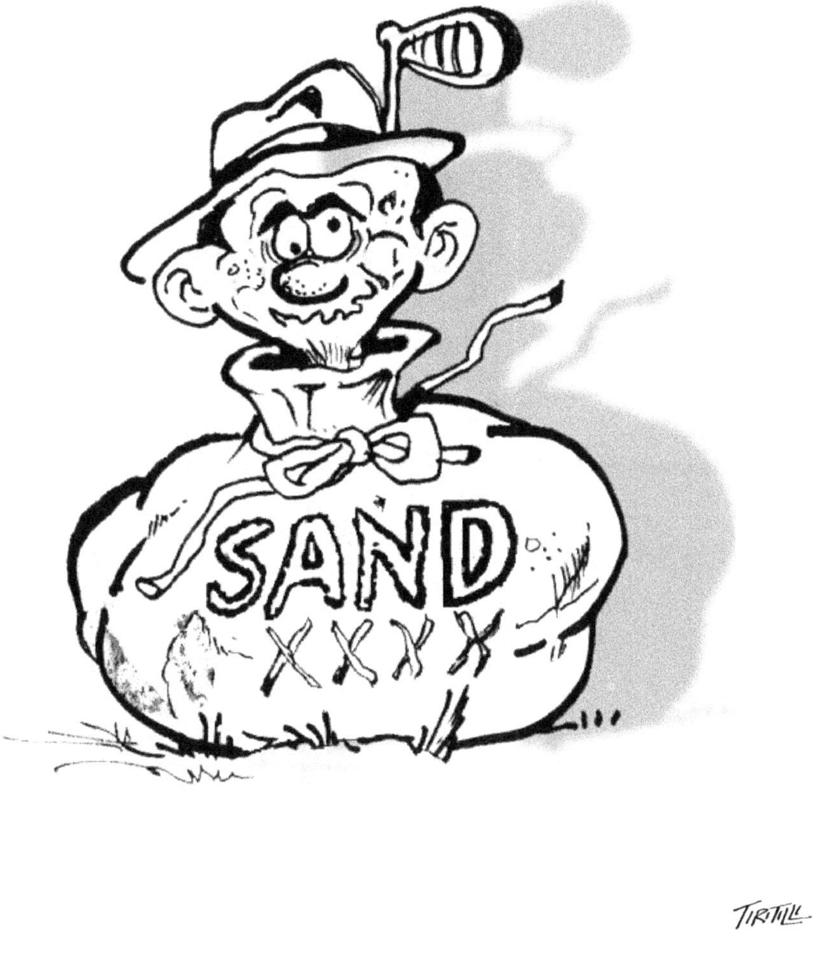
SAND
XXXX
TIRITILLI

Sandbagger

Scratch Golfer

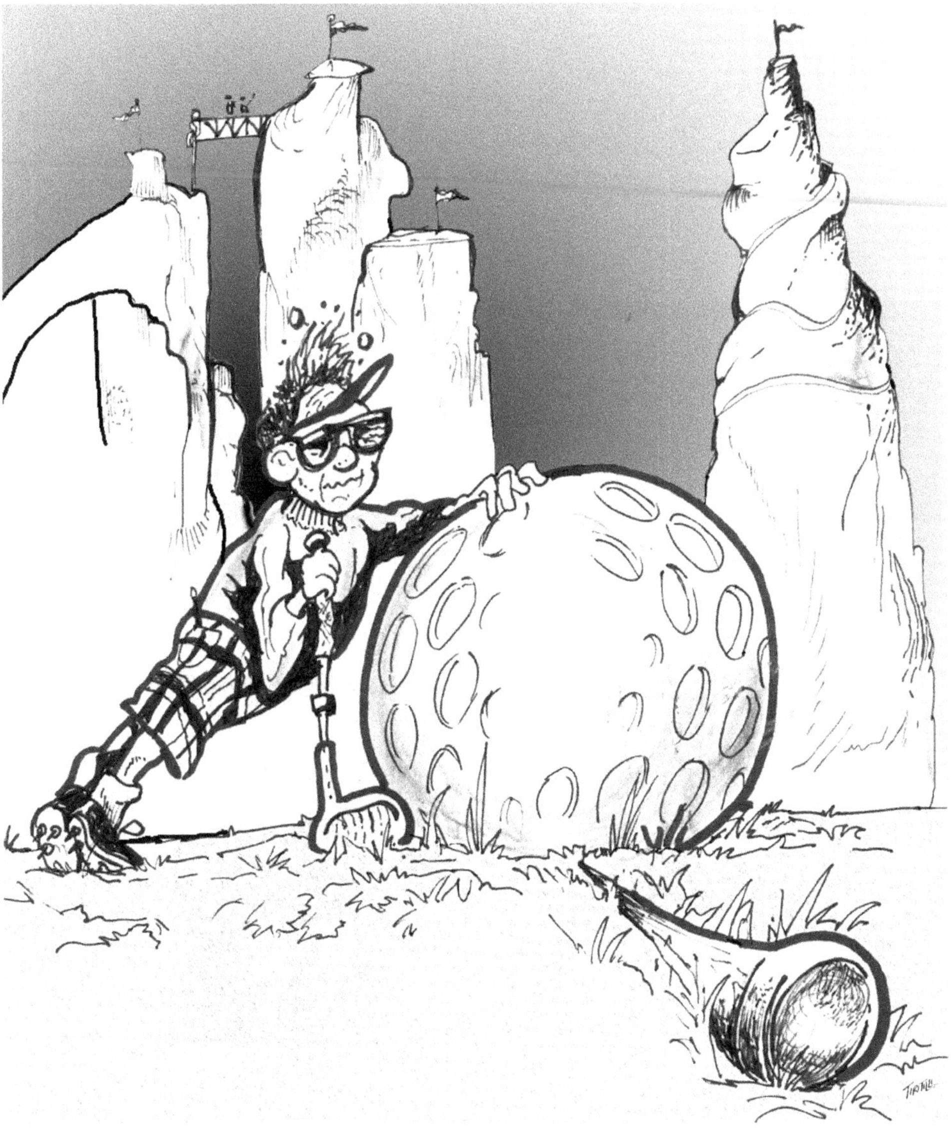

Extreme Golf

Future golf widow

Bird "E"

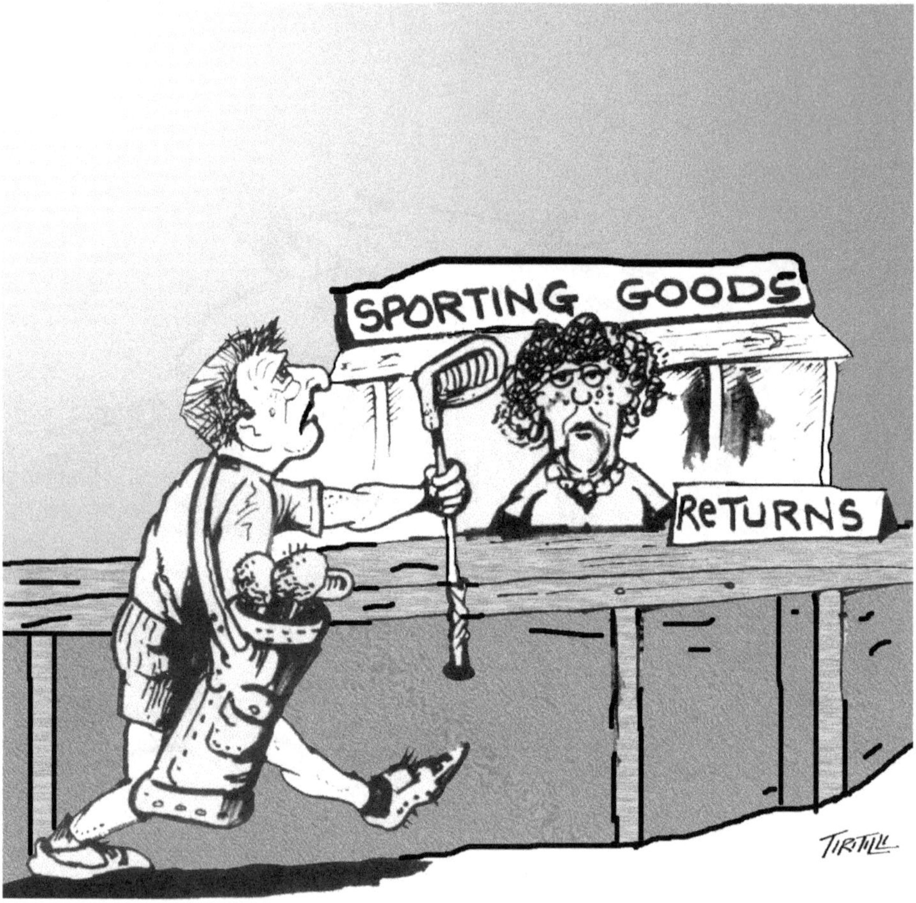
SPORTING GOODS
RETURNS
TIRITILLI

"It doesn't work!"

The Waggle

This goose, is goose, a goose, good goose, way goose, to goose, keep goose, a goose, golf goose, idiot goose, like goose, you goose, busy goose, for goose, 25 goose, seconds goose! ... Now read without the word goose.

_S-l-o-w_ Play

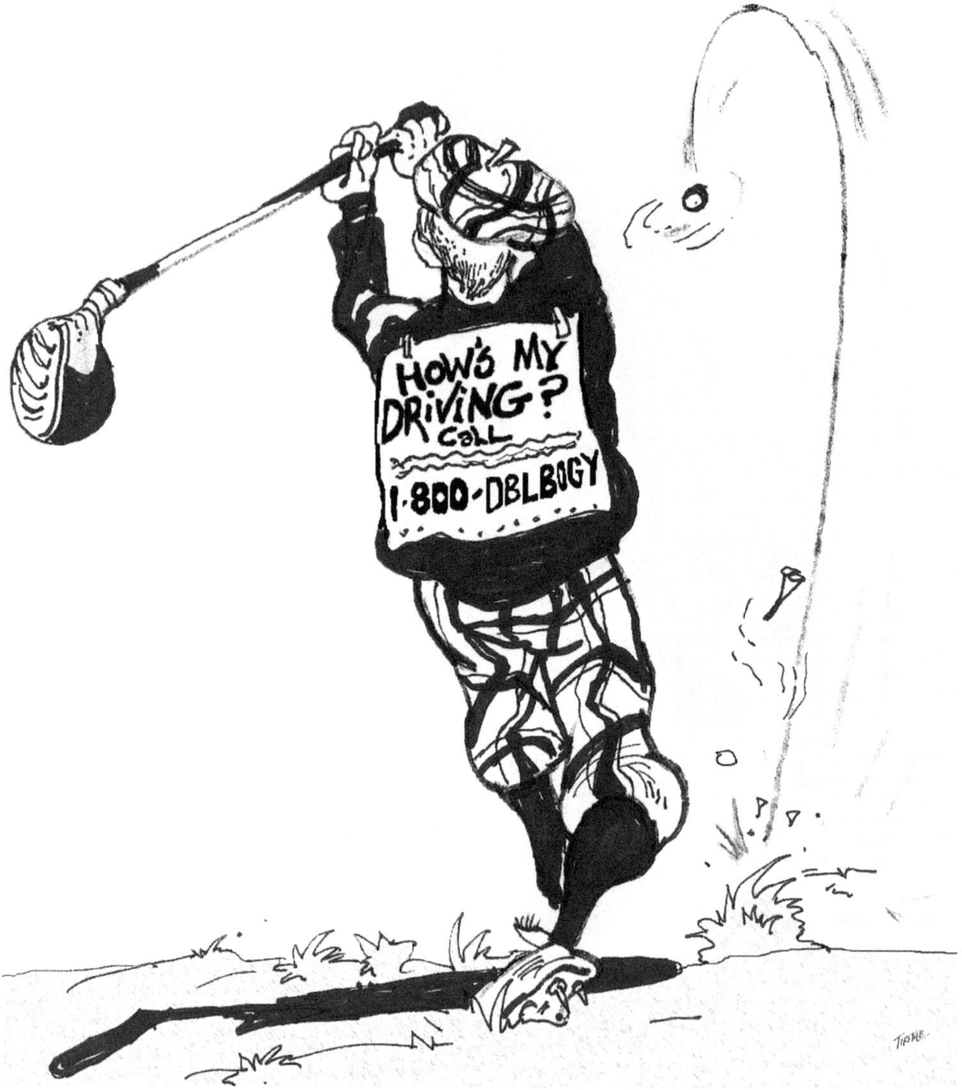
HOW'S MY DRIVING? CALL
1-800-DBLBOGY

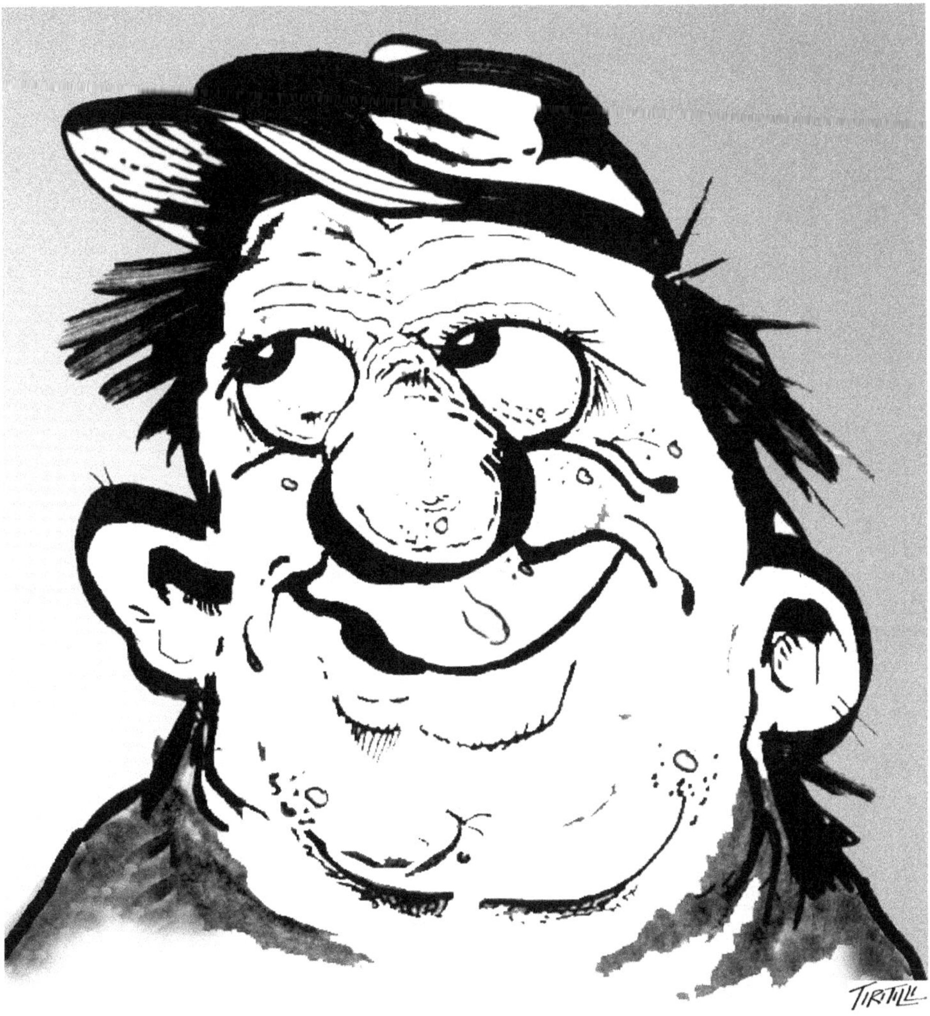
TIRITILLI

"Sorry, my 8 beats your 9!"

Who says you can't take it with you?

Golf is the only sport where the most feared opponent is...YOU!

" I have a club for every shot."

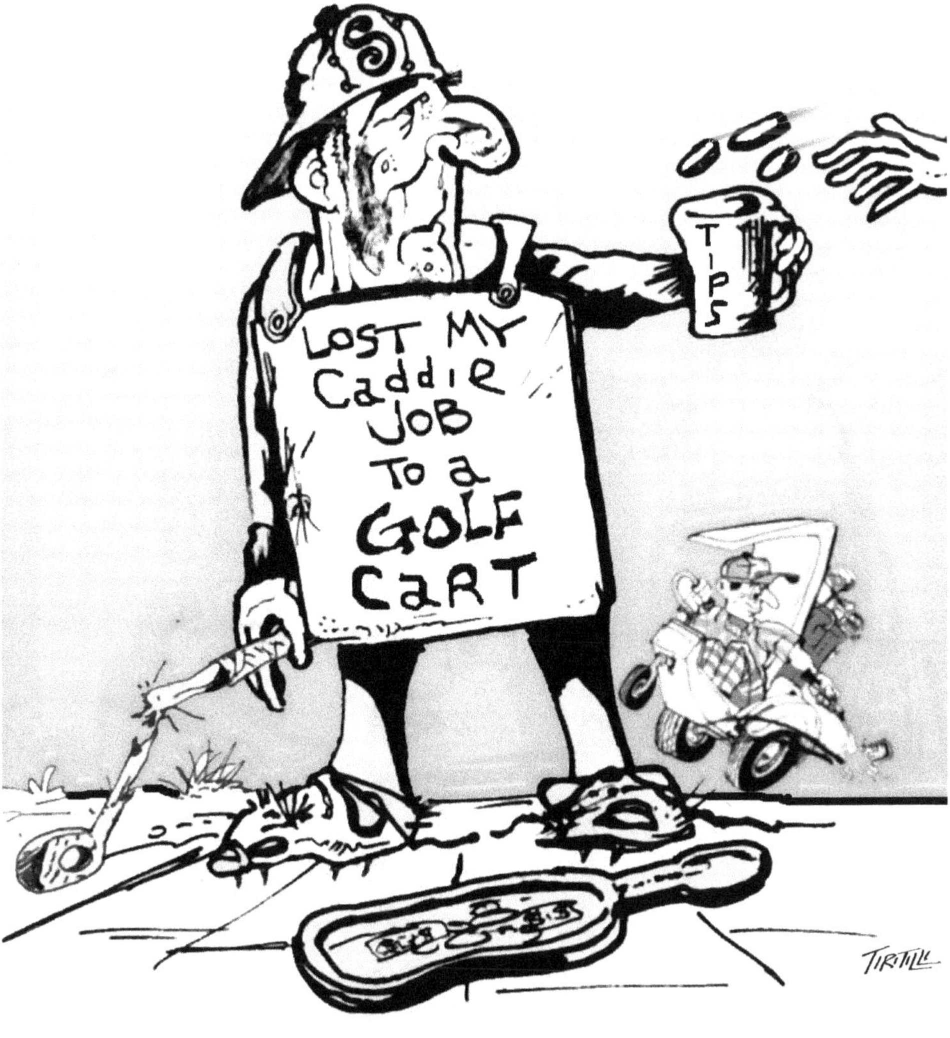
TIPS
LOST MY Caddie JOB To a GOLF CaRT
TIRITILLI

"I play in the low 80's.
If it's any hotter, I stay home."

"Your best shots in golf are
your practice swings."

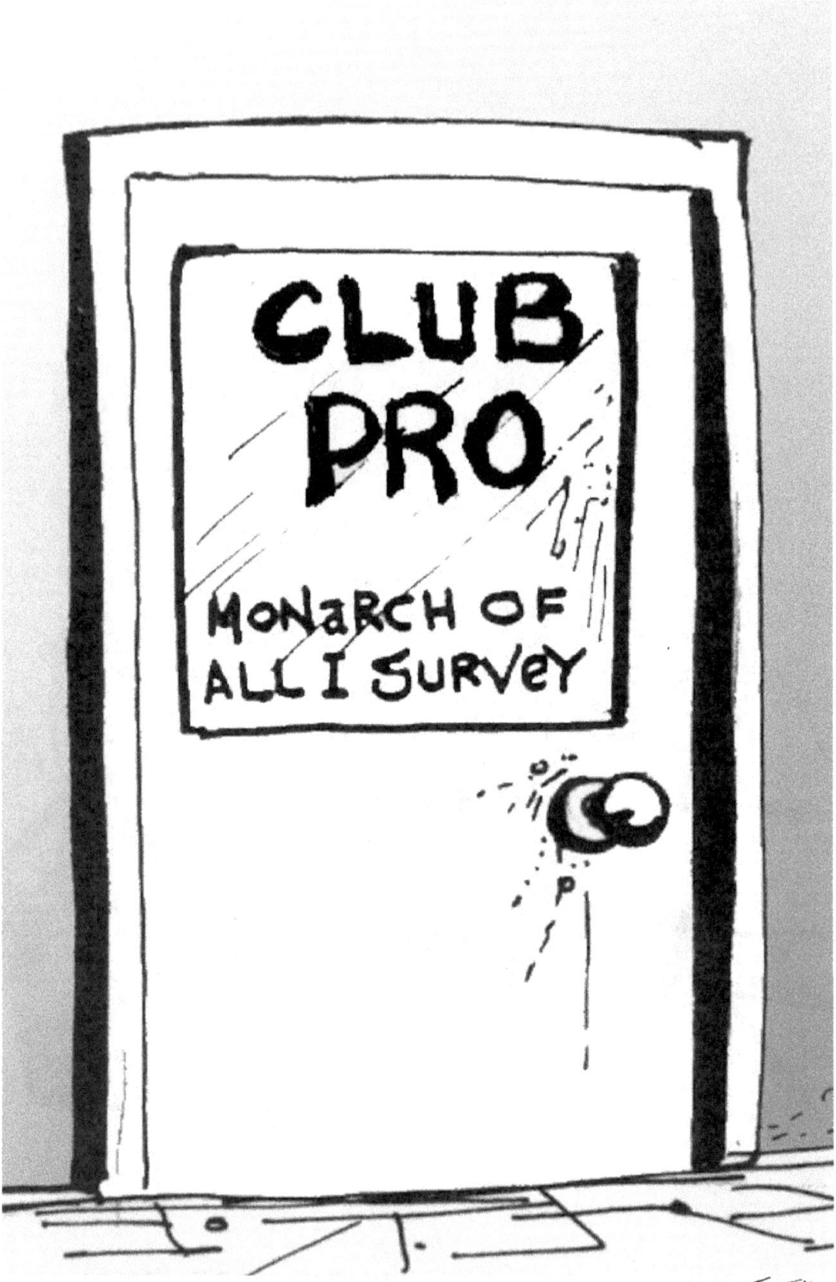
CLUB PRO
MONARCH OF ALL I SURVEY

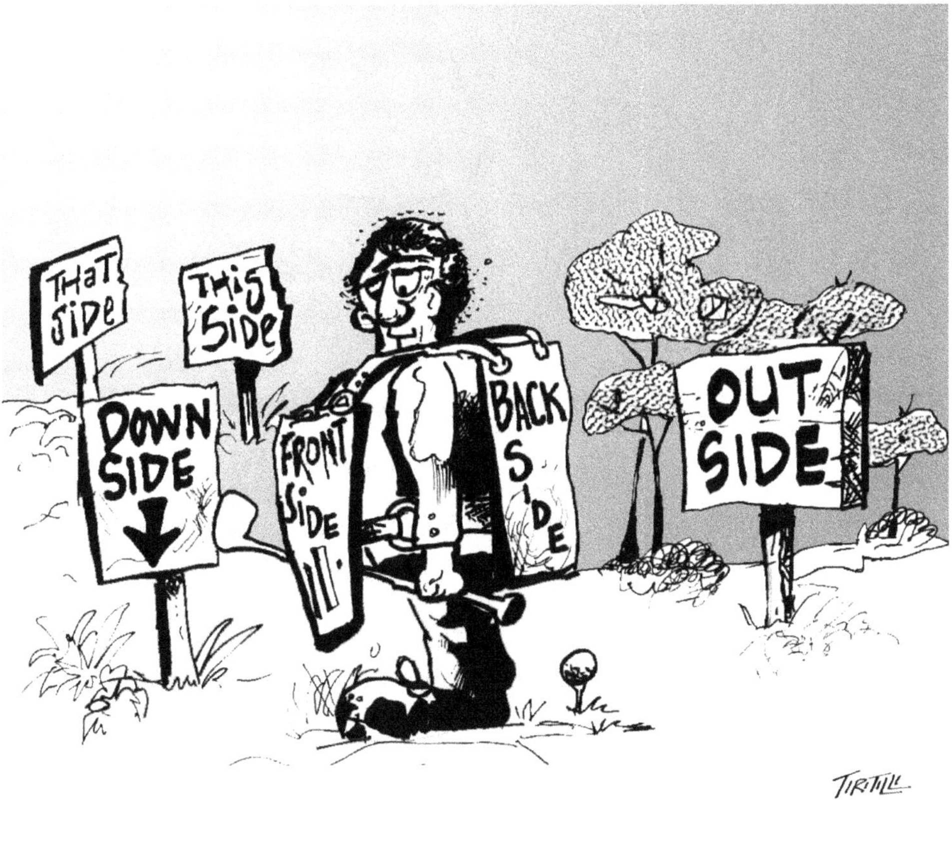
THAT SIDE
THIS SIDE
DOWN SIDE
FRONT SIDE
BACK SIDE
OUT SIDE
TIRITILLI

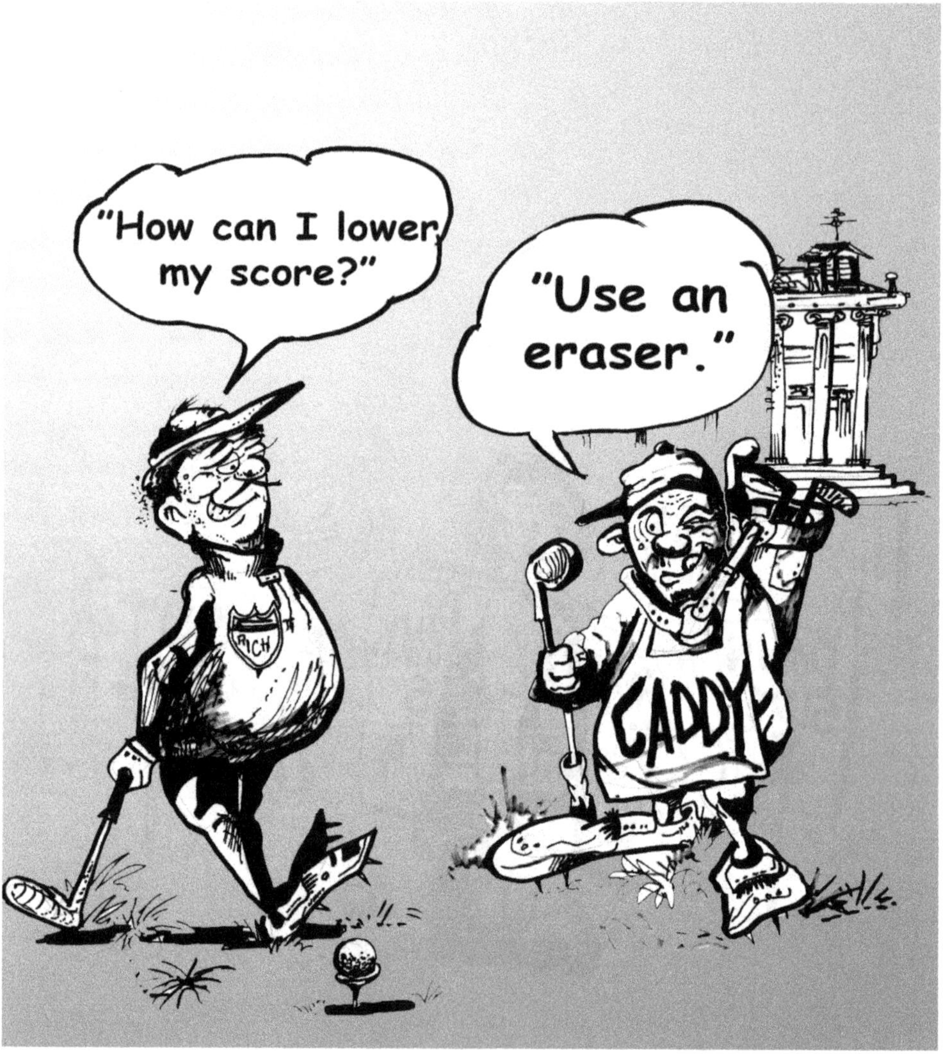
"How can I lower my score?"
"Use an eraser."
RICH
CADDY
TIRITILL

"Phil, what's the matter with you. Never pick-up your ball while its still moving!"

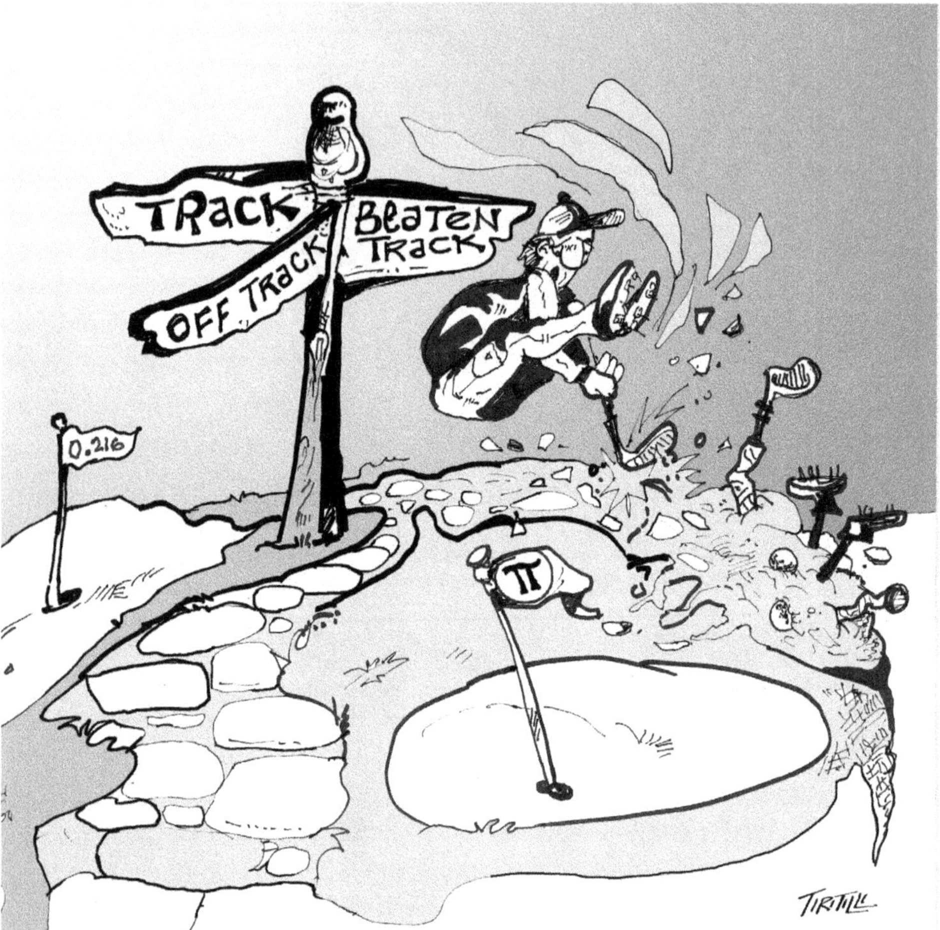
TRACK
BEATEN TRACK
OFF TRACK
0.216
π
TIRITILLI

"Honey, which do you prefer...
senior golf or ladies golf?"

51

"... and you're picking up my expenses."

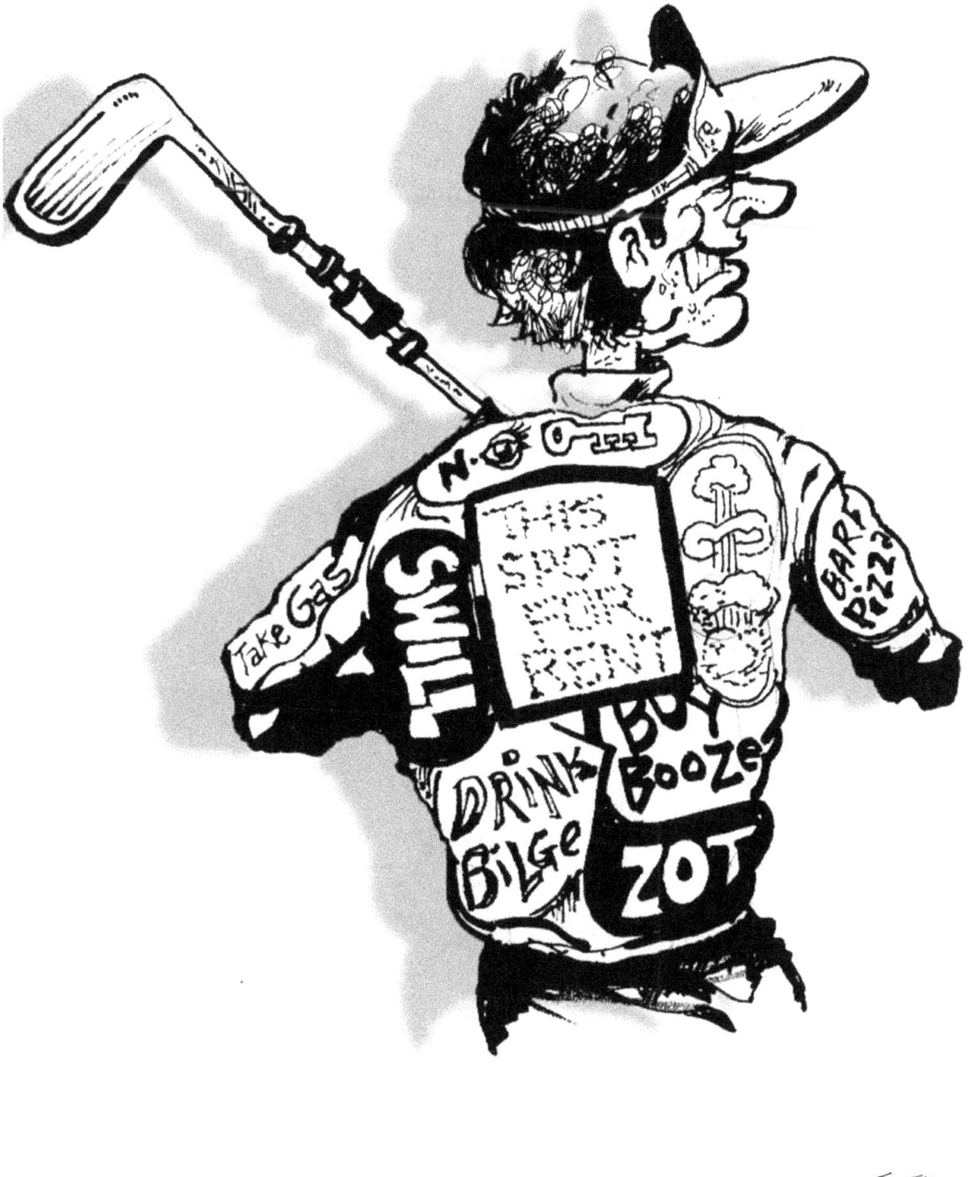
N
THIS SPOT FOR RENT
SWILL
Take Gas
BAR
Pizza
BUY Booze
DRINK Bilge
ZOT
TIRITILLI

Sponsor needed

Skin's game

**Head down,
eyes on the ball!**

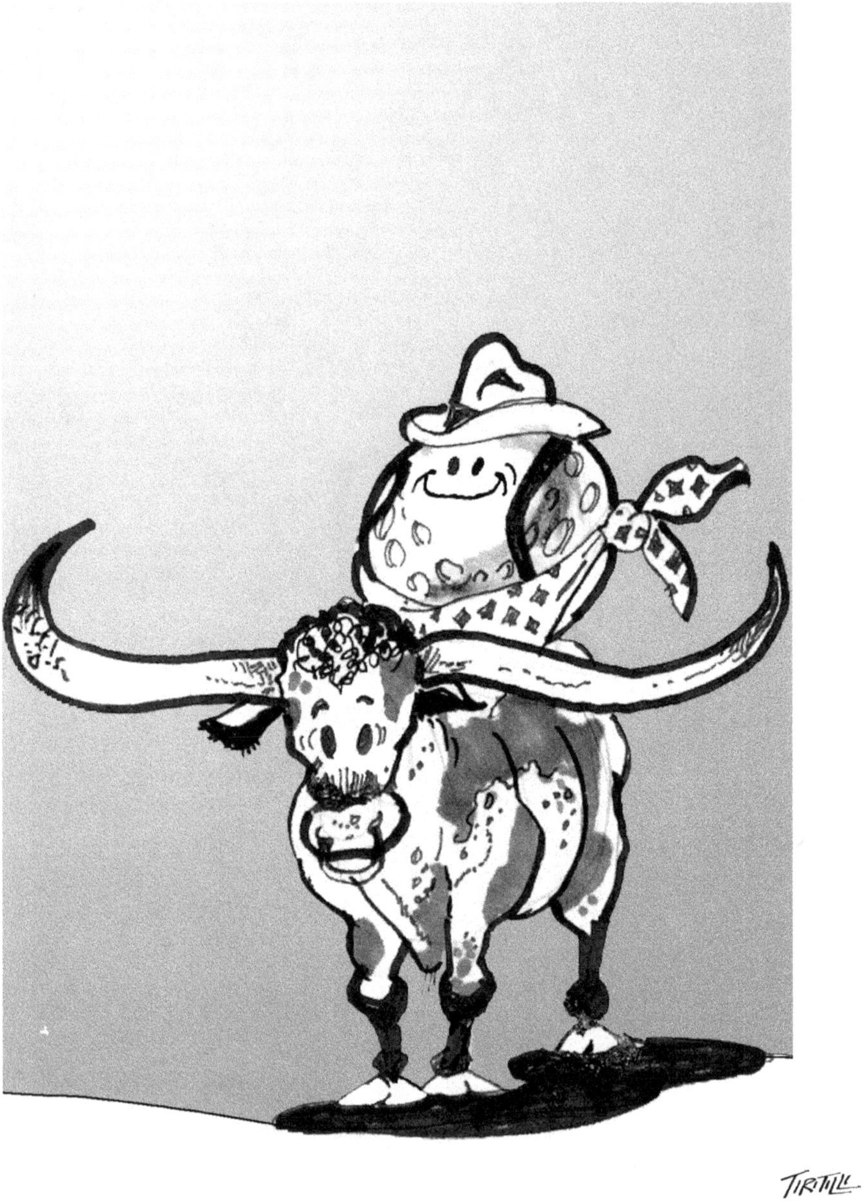
TIRITILLI

Range Ball

"Who said playing in the rain is fun?"

"Golf news is not FAKE news!"

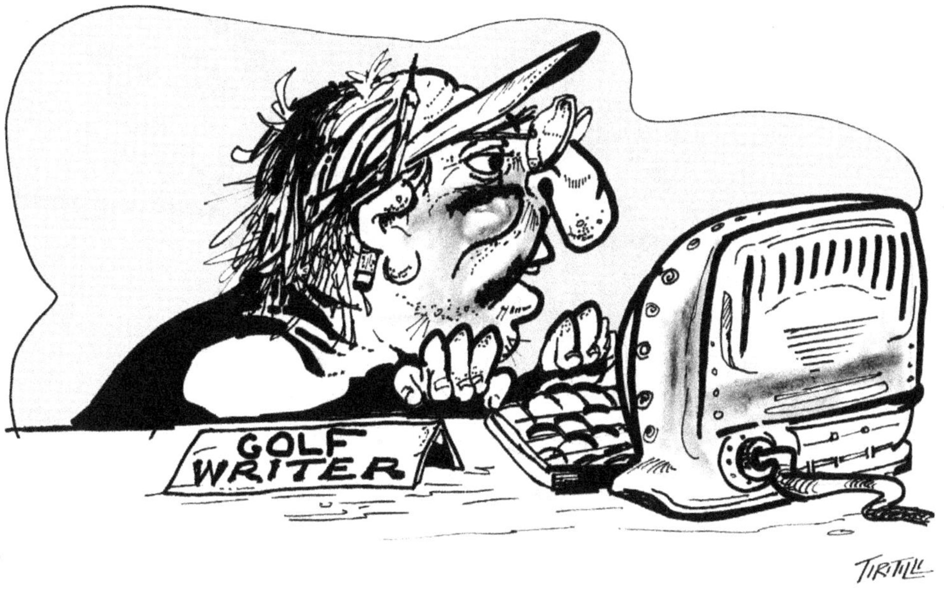
GOLF WRITER
TIRITILLI

"I don't write FAKE news!"

"It looks like he got a "4"on the last hole."

Dog-leg to the left.

"Actually, I love tennis more than golf!"

"It's either a cast for a broken golf shaft or a broken bat!"

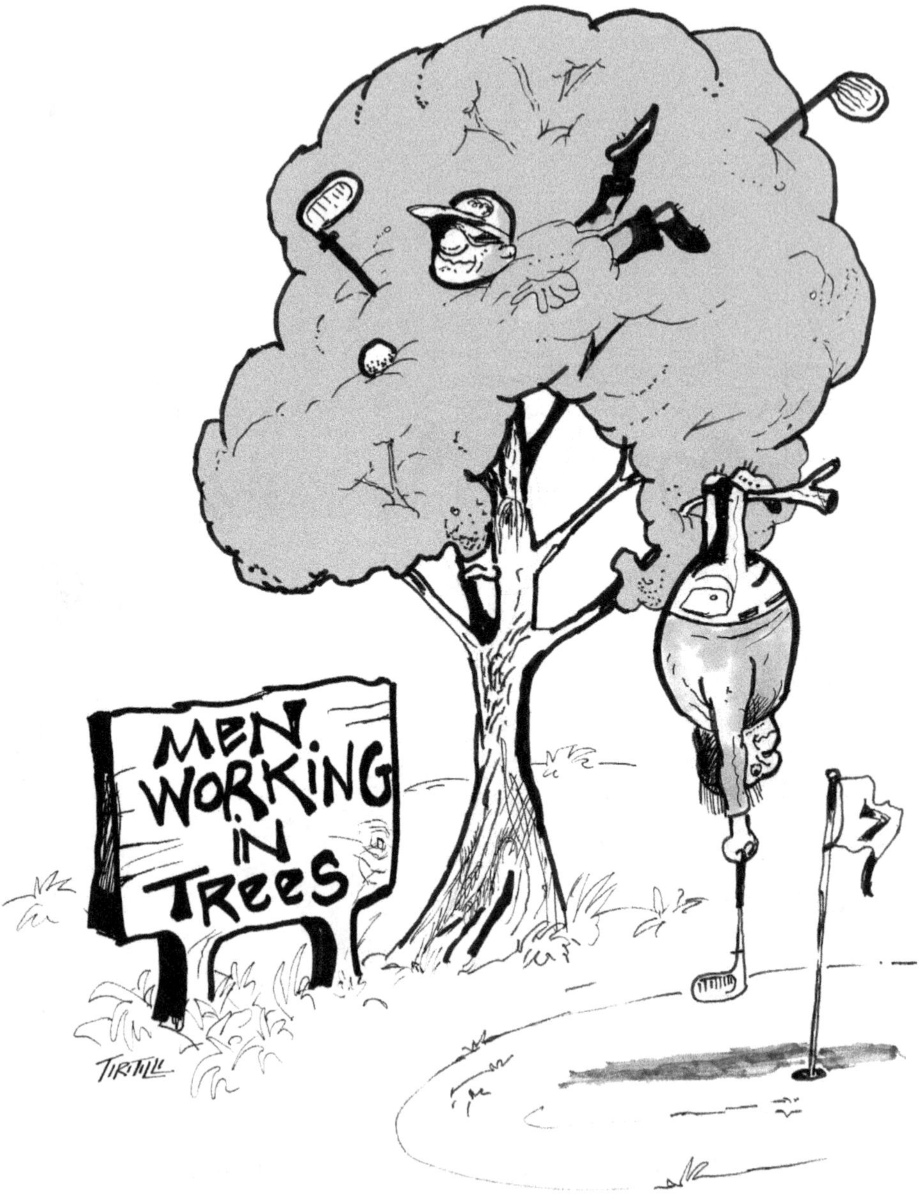
MEN WORKING iN TREES
TIRITILLI

**Only mad dogs and Englishmen
go out in the midday sun.**

"Looks like almost everyone
is on the disabled list."

**"This pill will make you
hit the ball 350 yards!"**

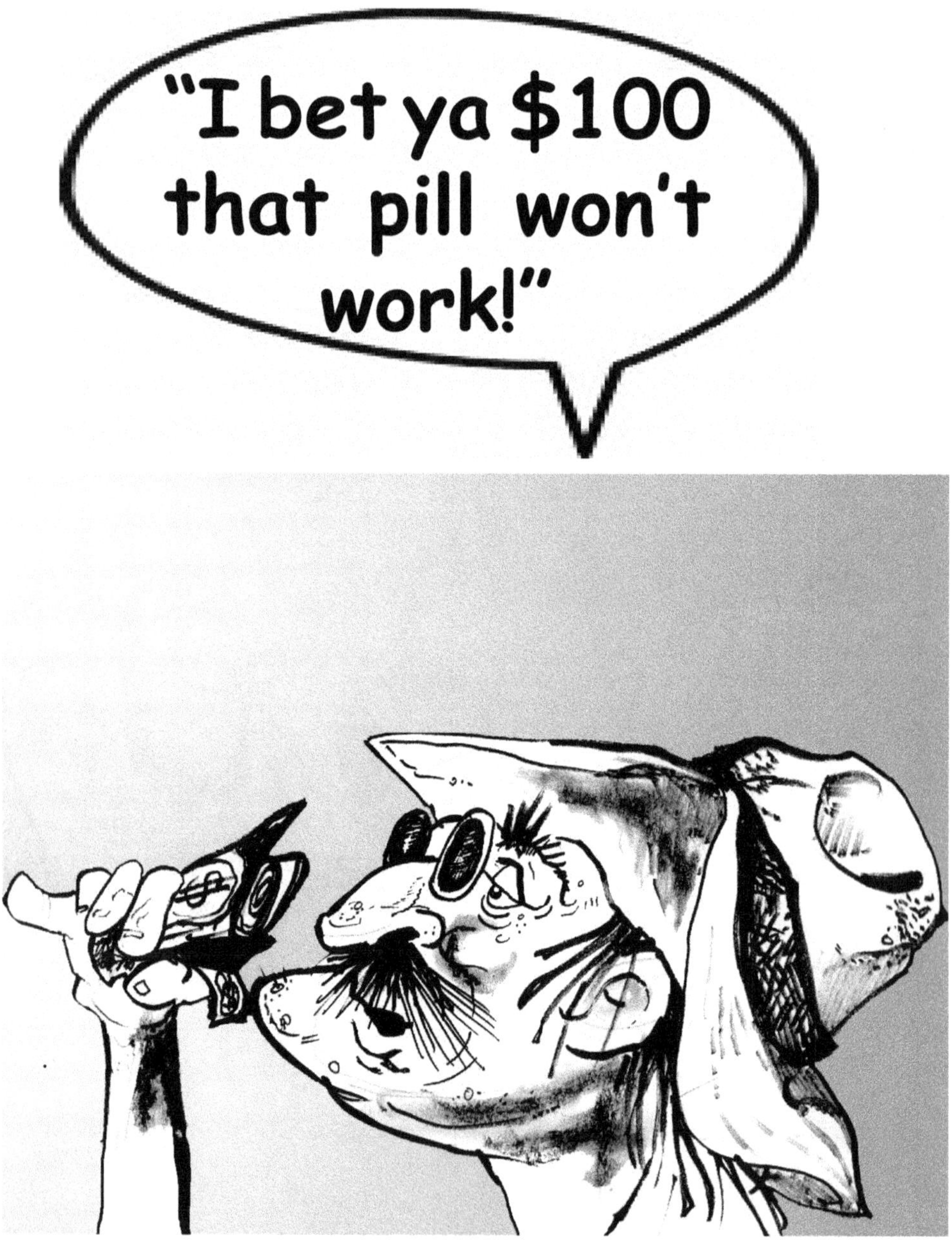
"I bet ya $100 that pill won't work!"
TIRITILLI

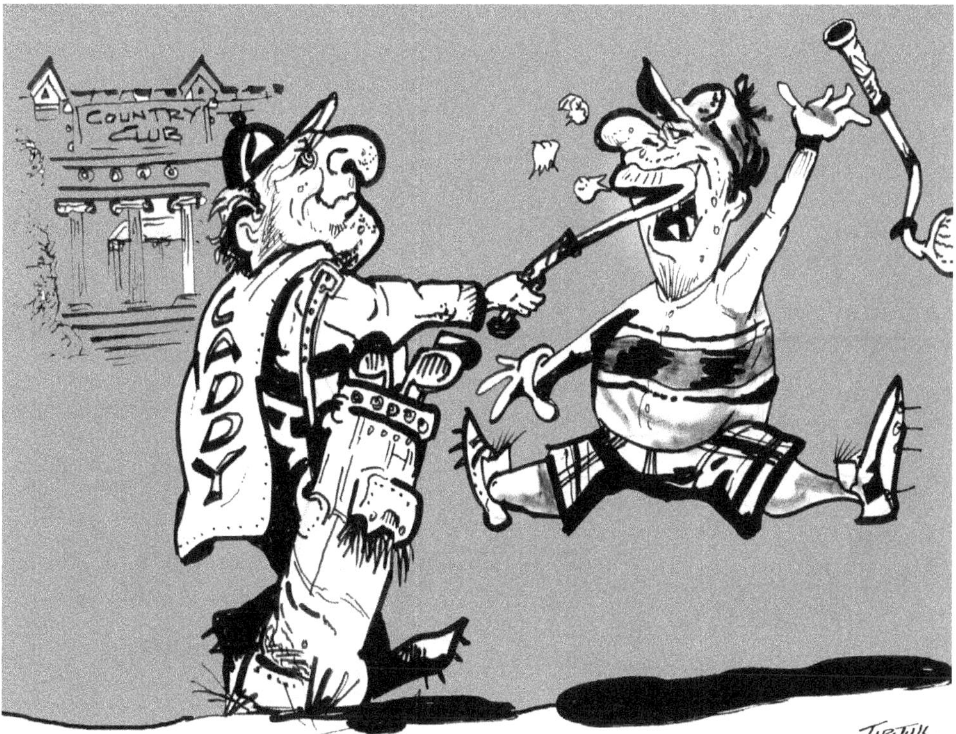
COUNTRY CLUB
CADDY

Club sandwich

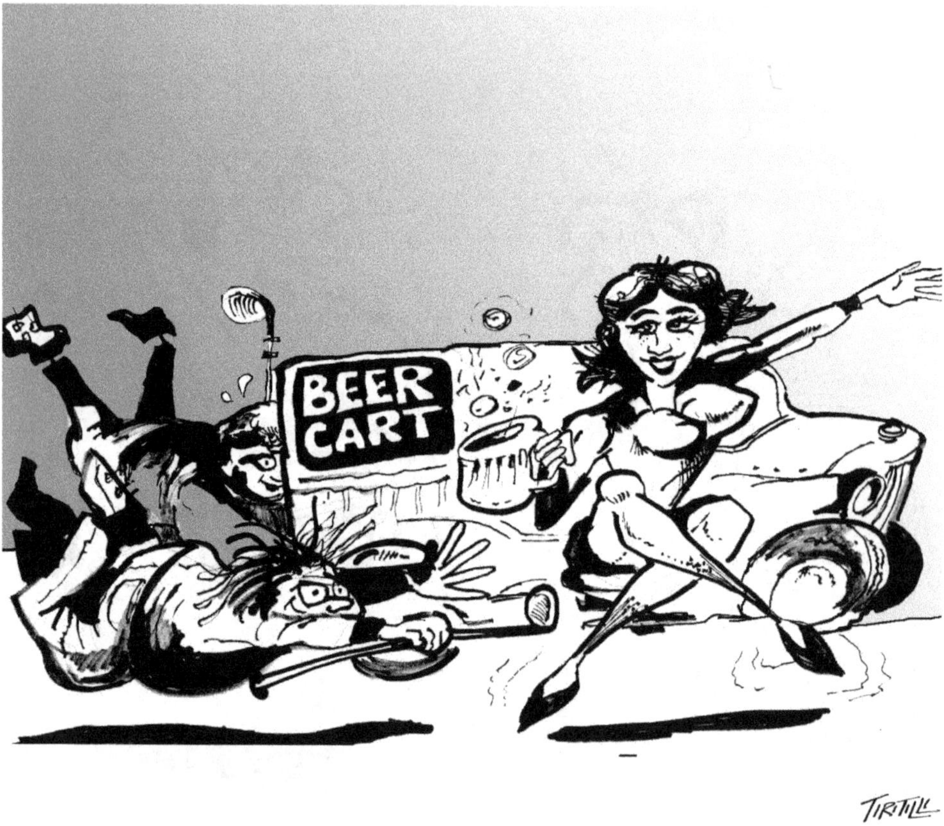
BEER
CART
TIRITILLI

"Get HUMPED!"

**"FORE professor!
You put our tee-times
inside the golf time machine!"**

... and I designed Carnoustie, Muirfield, Royal Troon, Pebble Beach, Riviera, Augusta National and many more.

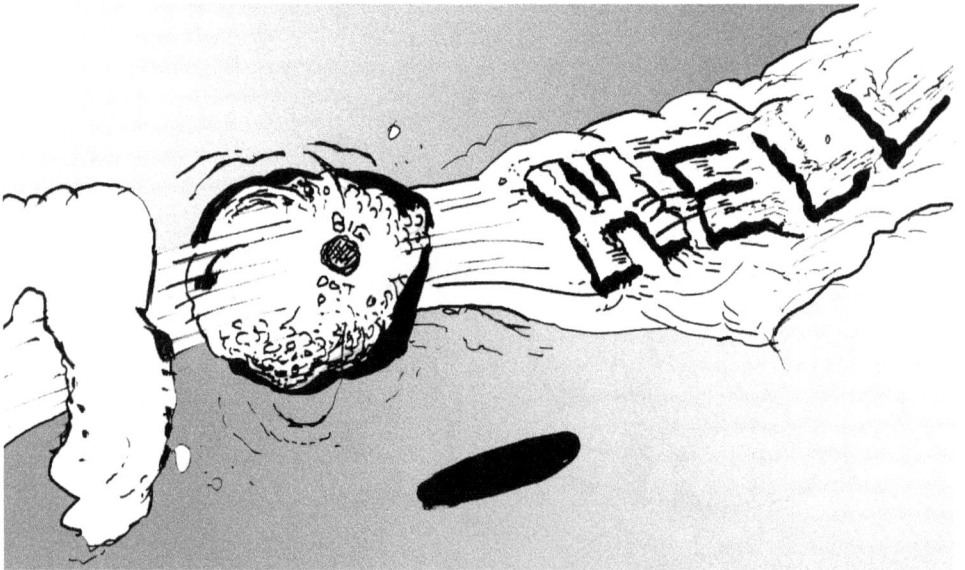

**Knocking the "HELL"
out of a golf ball!**

The "PERFECT" swing

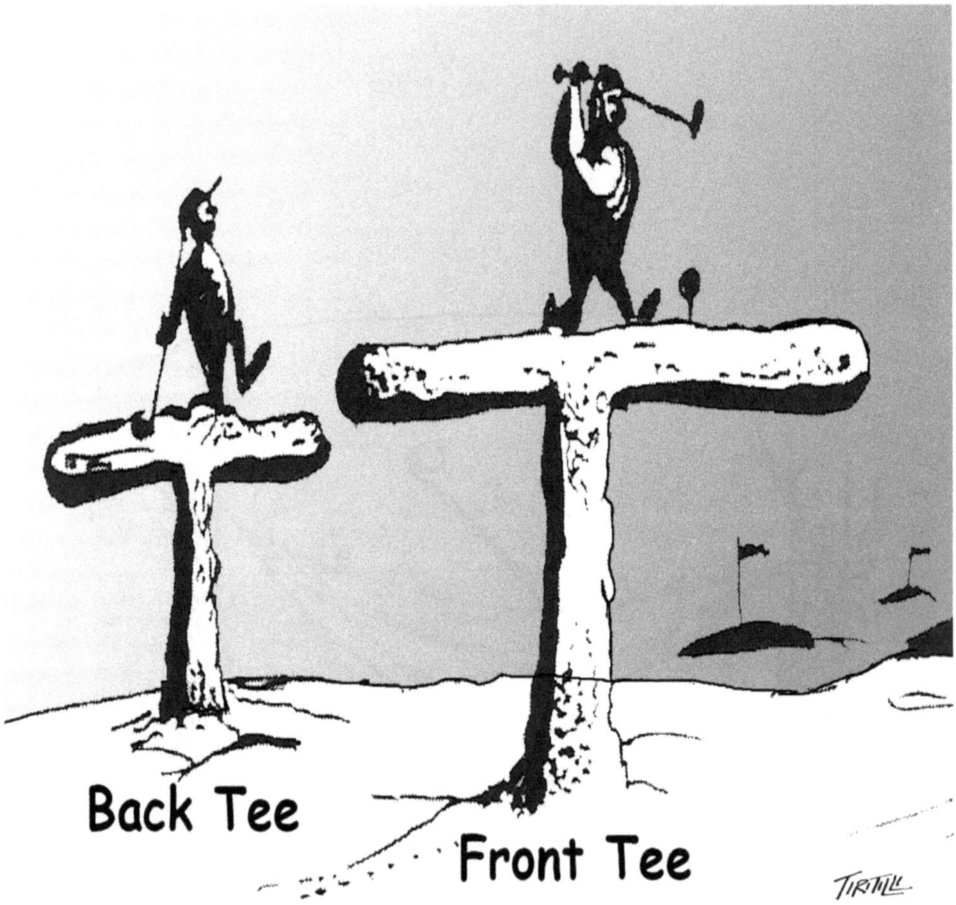
Back Tee
Front Tee
TIRITILLI

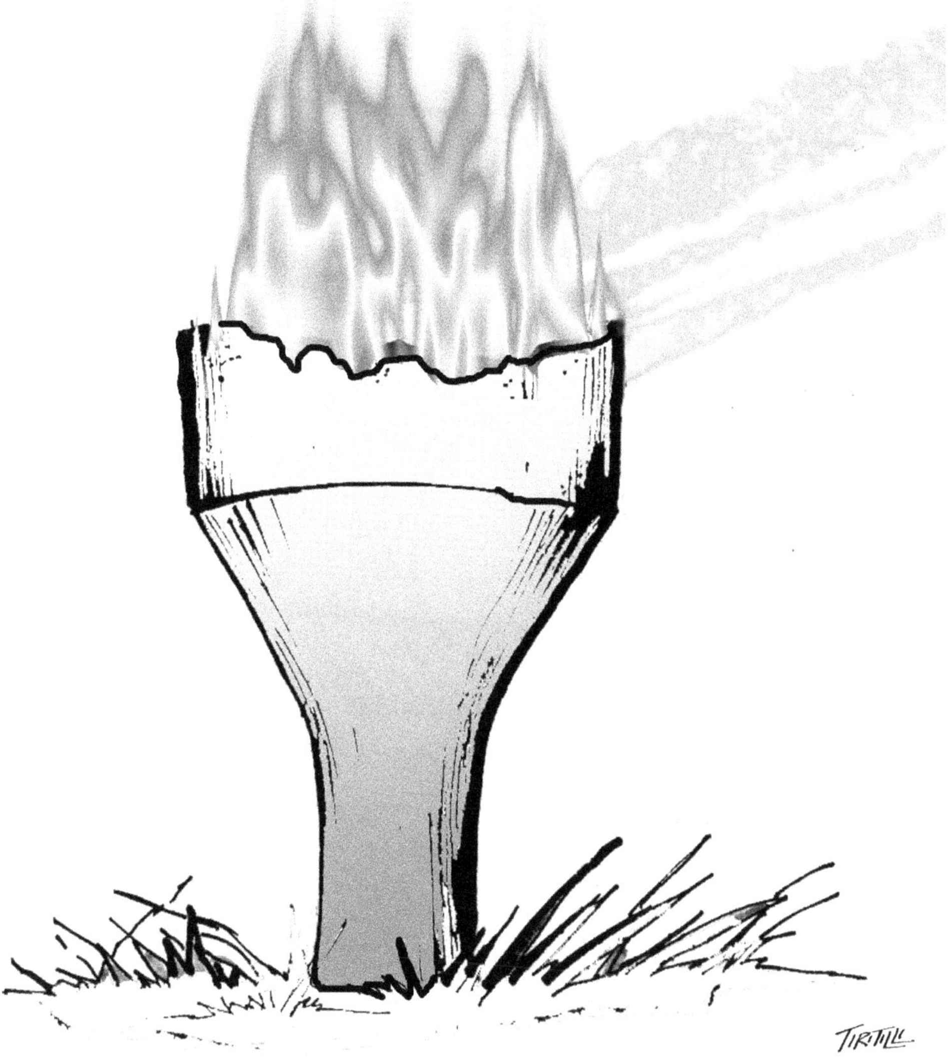
TIRITILLI

Hot off the tee

Golf Nut

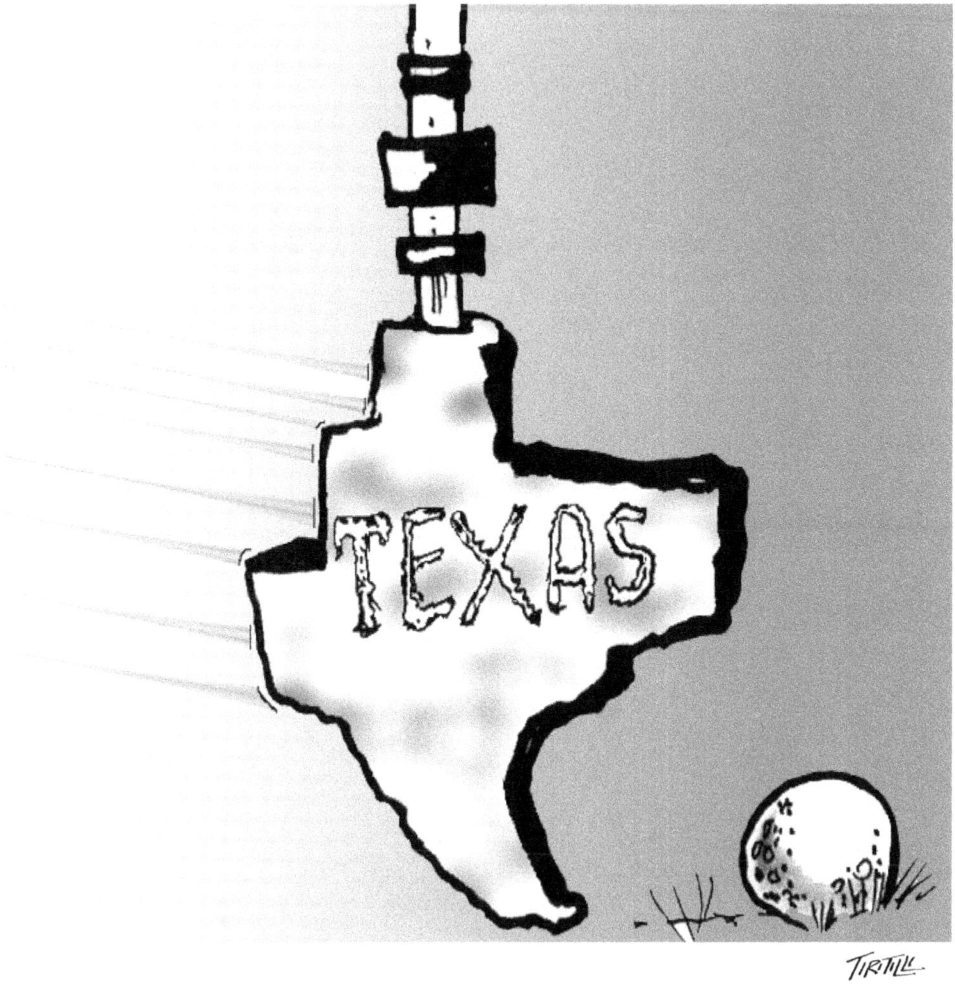
TEXAS
TIRITILLI

Texas Wedge

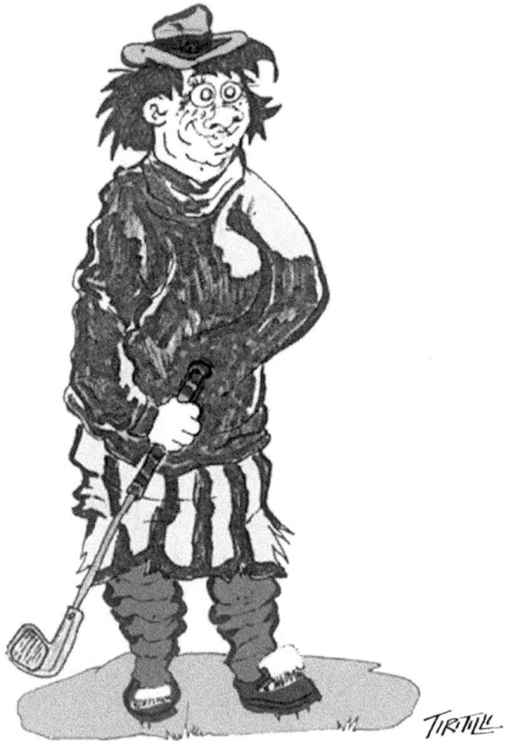
TIRITILLI

Golf Bag

"Sir, your tee-time is in 15 minutes."

"Will you stop clowning around!"

At the rule's committee meeting

Michealangelo creates "GOD"...
GOD creates GOLF!

84

"Don't you know that golfers don't understand Quantum Mechanics?"

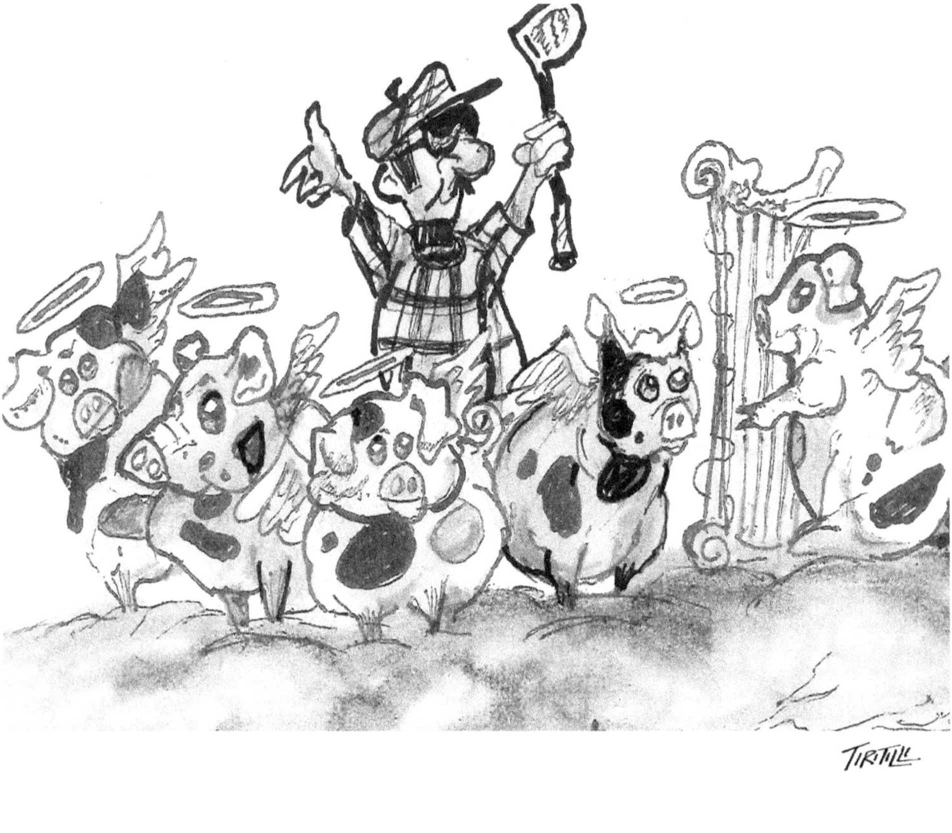
TIRITILLI

Golf's HOG HEAVEN

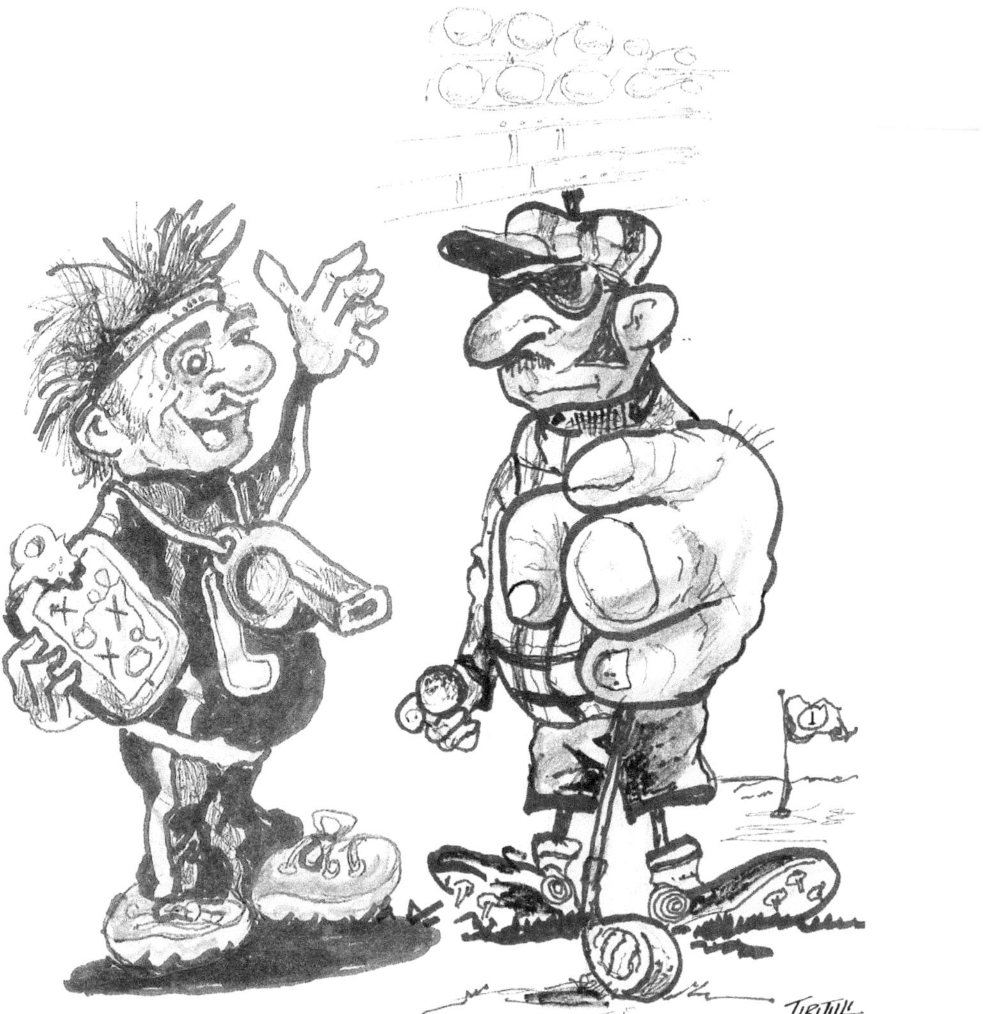
TIRITILLI

"I like the name LEFTY!"

"Free DROP! Free DROP! One more DROP and I'll be going coconuts!"

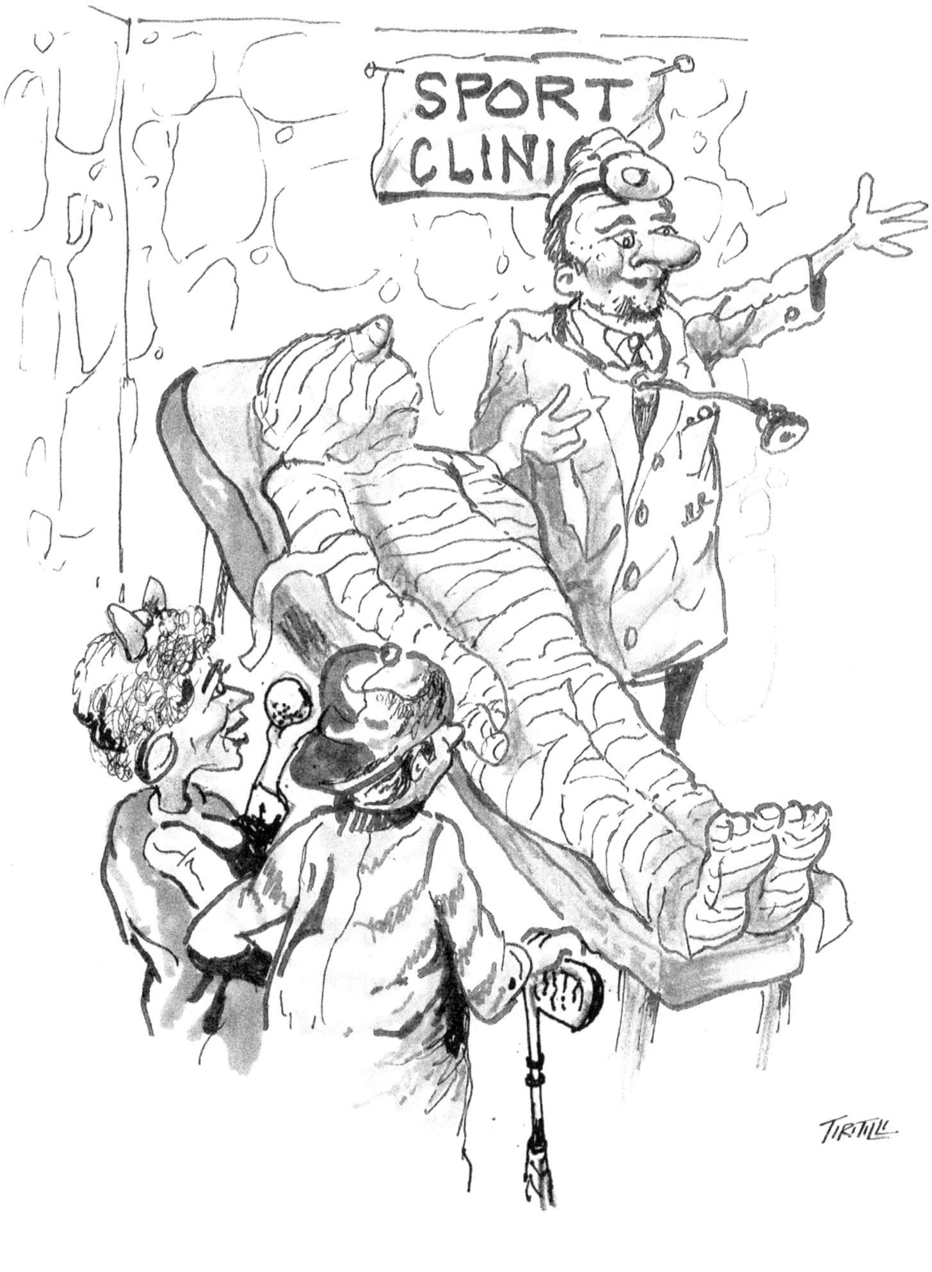
SPORT
CLINI
TIRTILLI

"OK Guys... it's a WRAP!"

"Mr. President, we will allow you to take only one mulligan per hole."

"It says... no man is an island!"

"No Johnny, only God can take three!"

**Chip misses final putt in the Masters...
goes to HELL in a hand basket!**

**"Told you it might be hotter
than Florida!"**

"I should have taken up tennis instead of golf!"

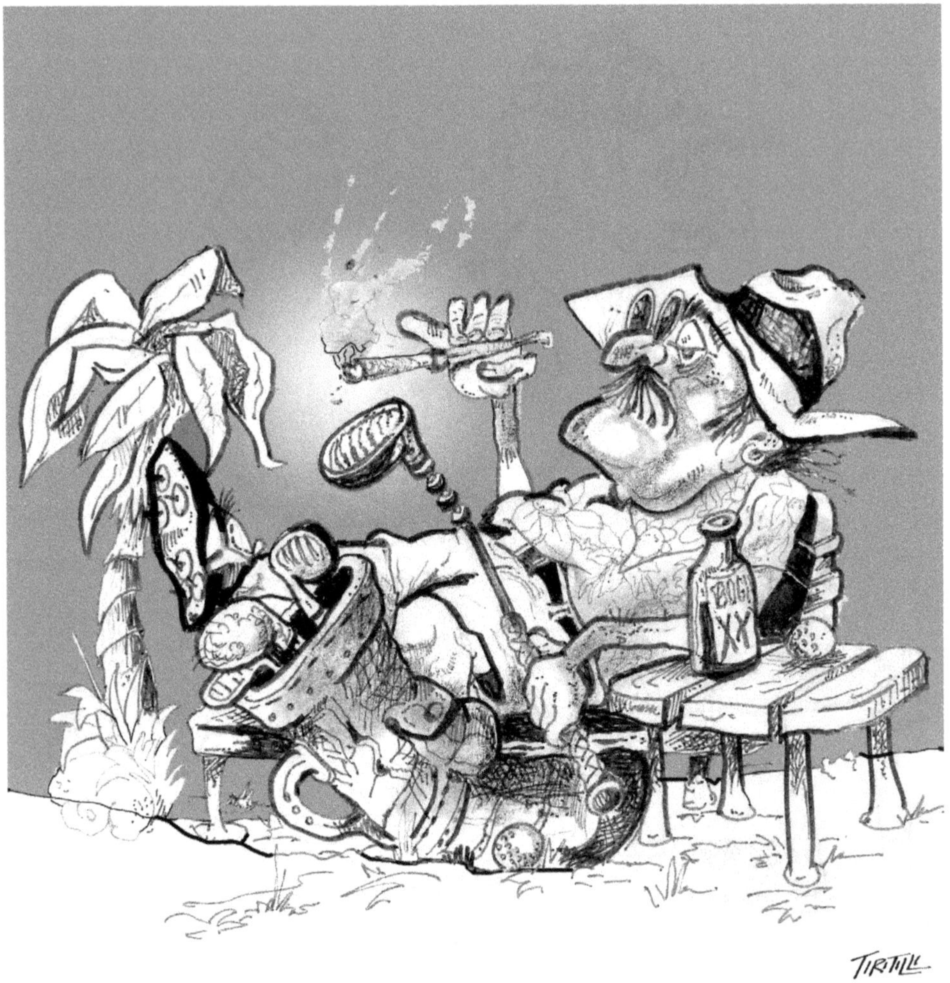
XX

“If you can’t win... CHEAT!”

Early Scottish Golf

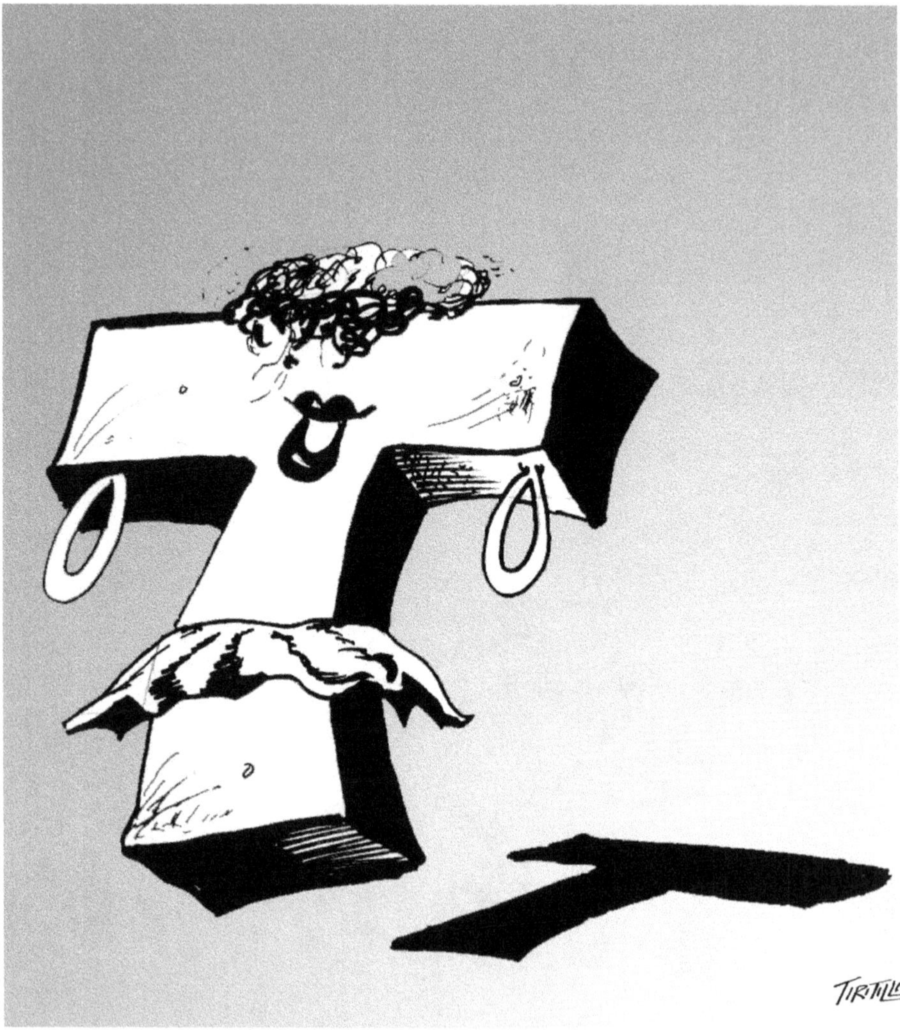
TIRITILLI

Ladies Tee

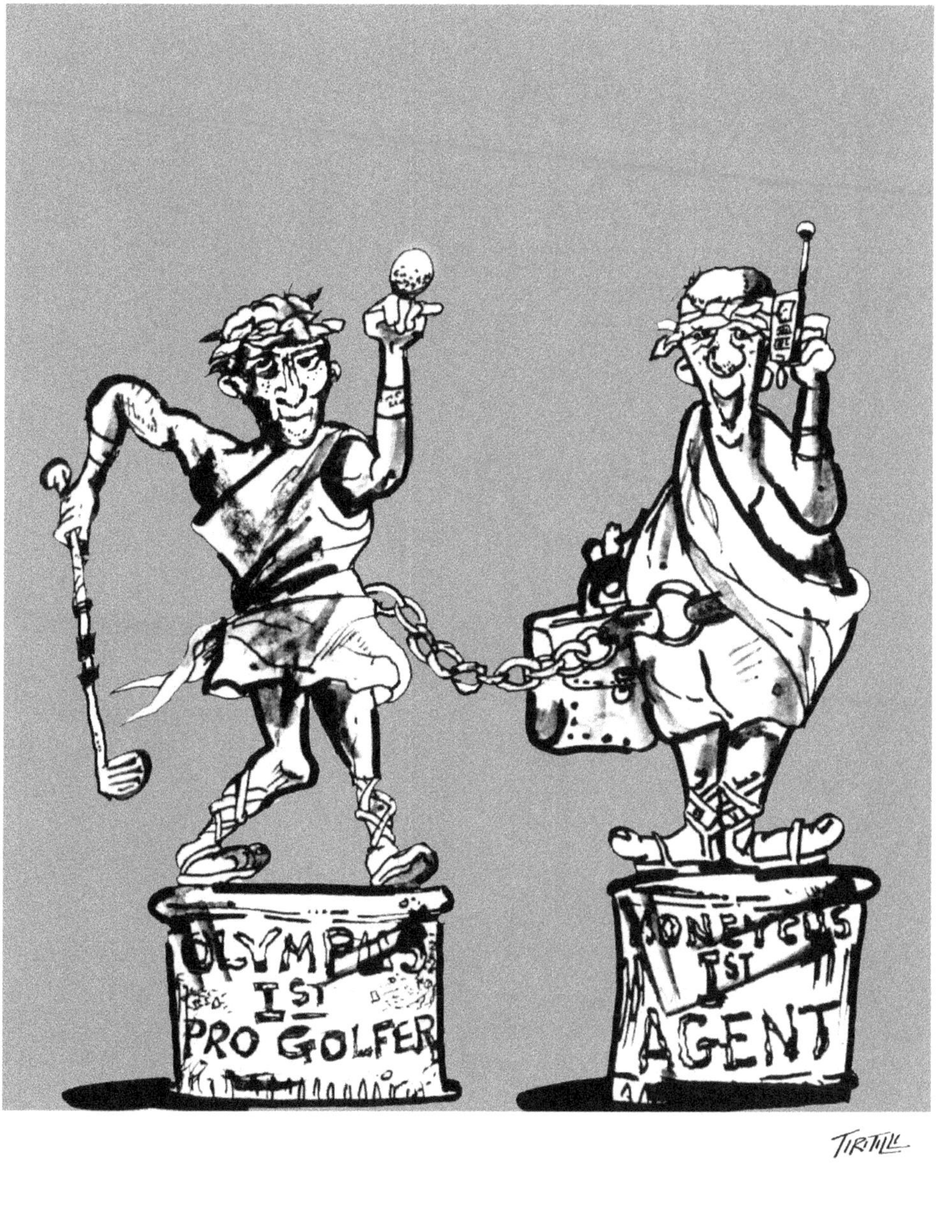
1ST
PRO GOLFER
1ST
AGENT
TIRITILLI

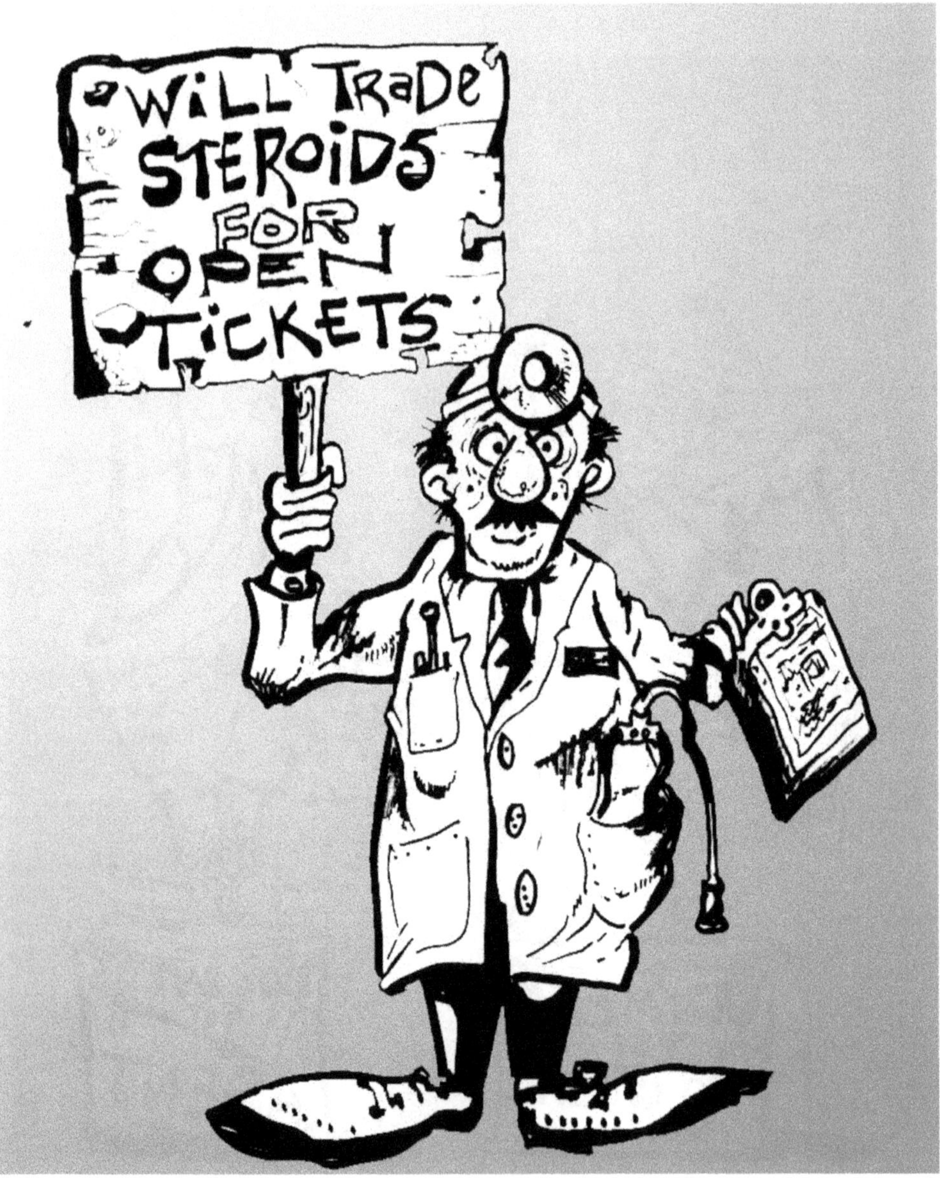
WILL TRADE
STEROIDS
FOR
OPEN
TICKETS

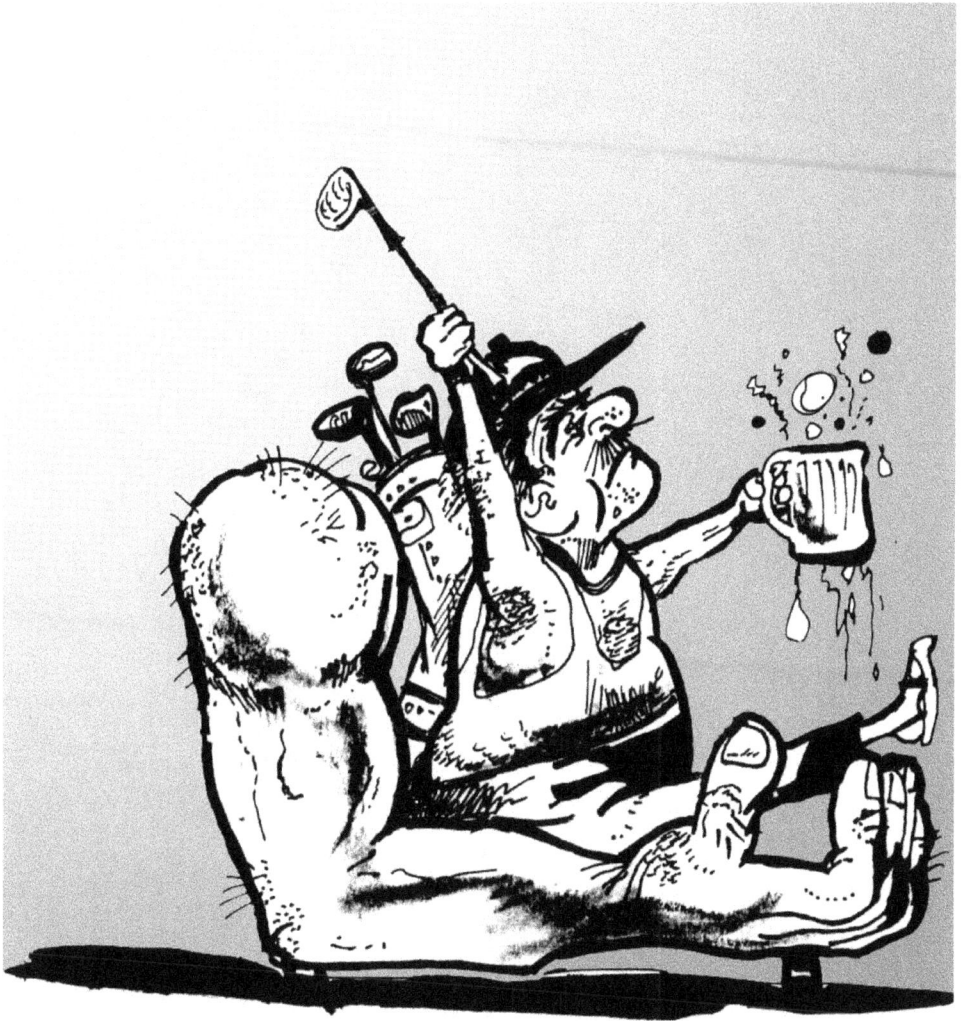

Arm chair golf fan

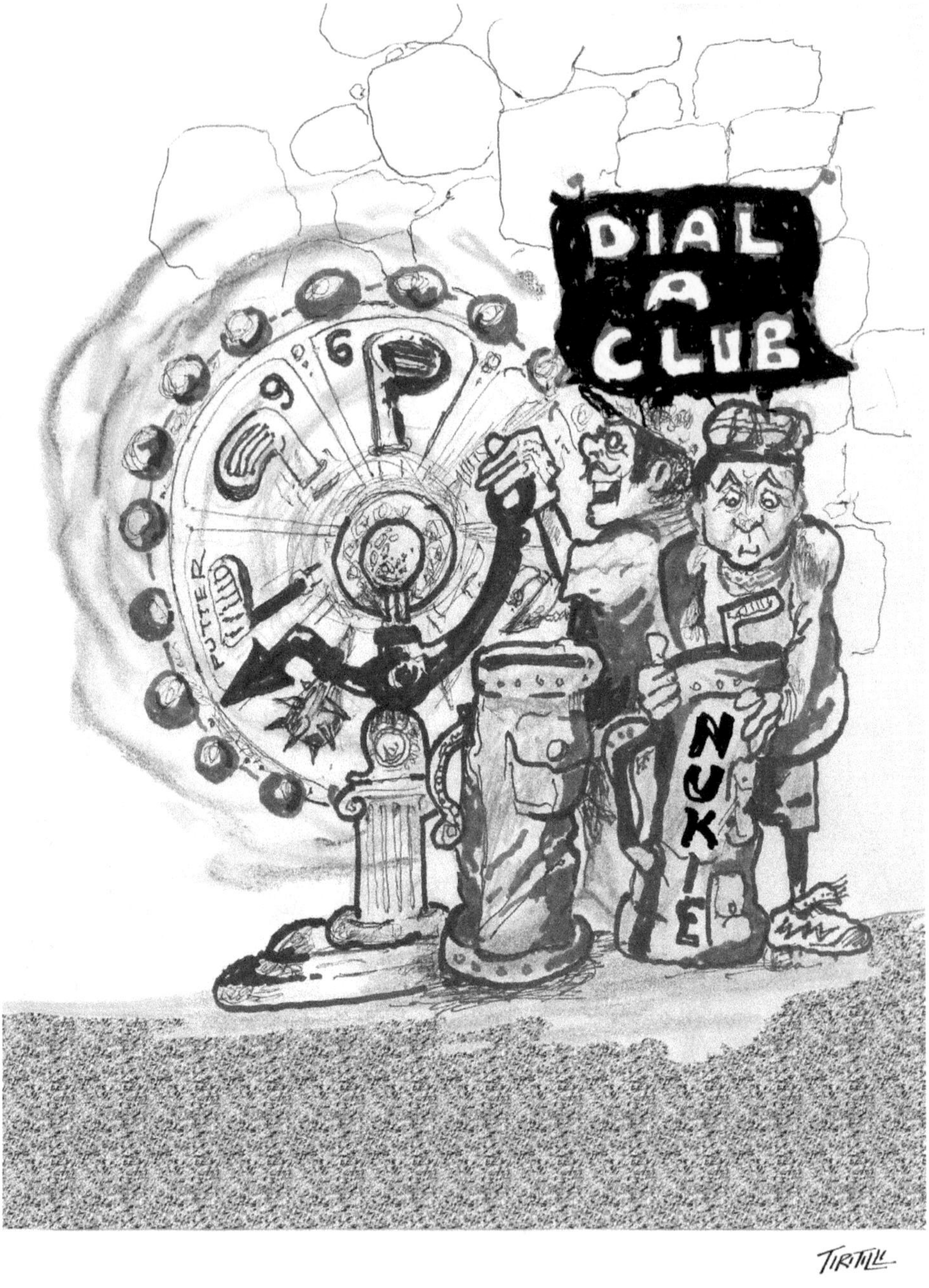
DIAL
A
CLUB
PUTTER
NUKIE
TIRITILLI

Golfer's Aid

"This does make the game harder!"

"Have you ever thought
about playing golf?"

"Listen, kid...
you gotta sign the contract, or else!"

**Sport losers are doomed
to the rath of HELL's BELLS!**

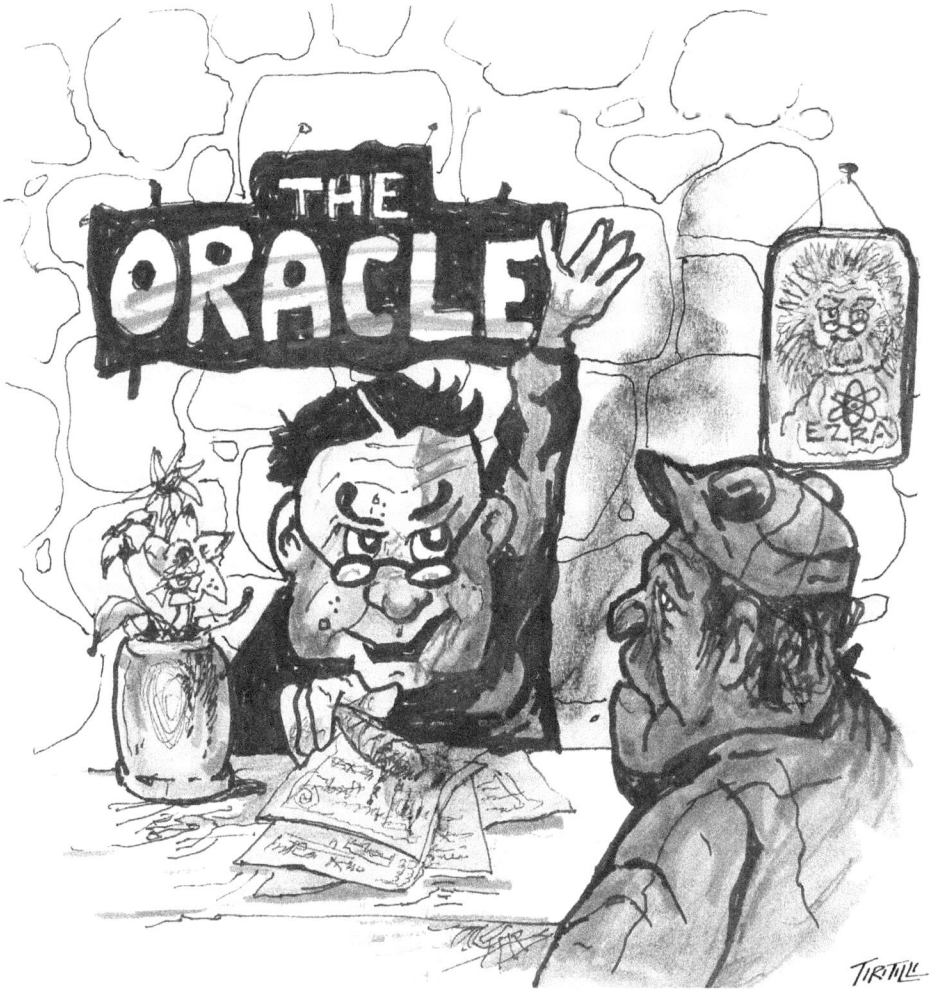

"Nobody in golf
should be considered a genius.
A genius is a guy like Ezra Einstein!"

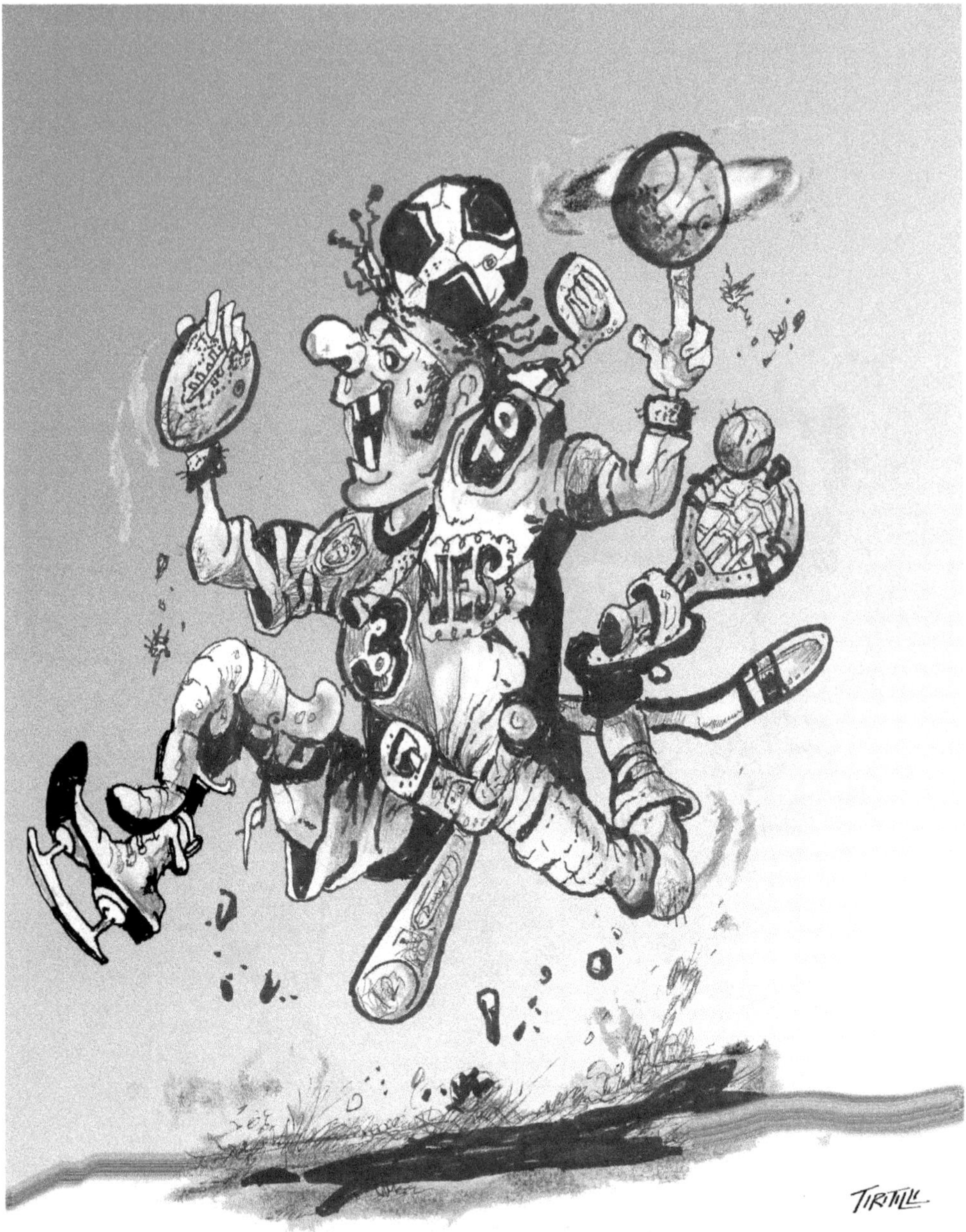

Mr. Sports!

"I'm not perfect,
but I'm perfect for your golf team."

"I start exercising at six o'clock in the morning NO MATTER what time is."

**"I'm going to graduate on time
NO matter how long it takes!"**

"Don't fret! You're just like Einstein. He got D's in college. He also got F's."

"Sports are the devil's playground.
except for golf!"

**Golfers must learn
to think outside the box!**

**"Your drives will get shorter
and your putts will get longer!"**

"So... you want to play around, huh?"

116

"I don't think you are
quite ready for the pro tour."

**The only way to consider golf
as exercise is to use a bowling ball.**

"The average golfer consumes twenty gallons of beer a year, but not all at once."

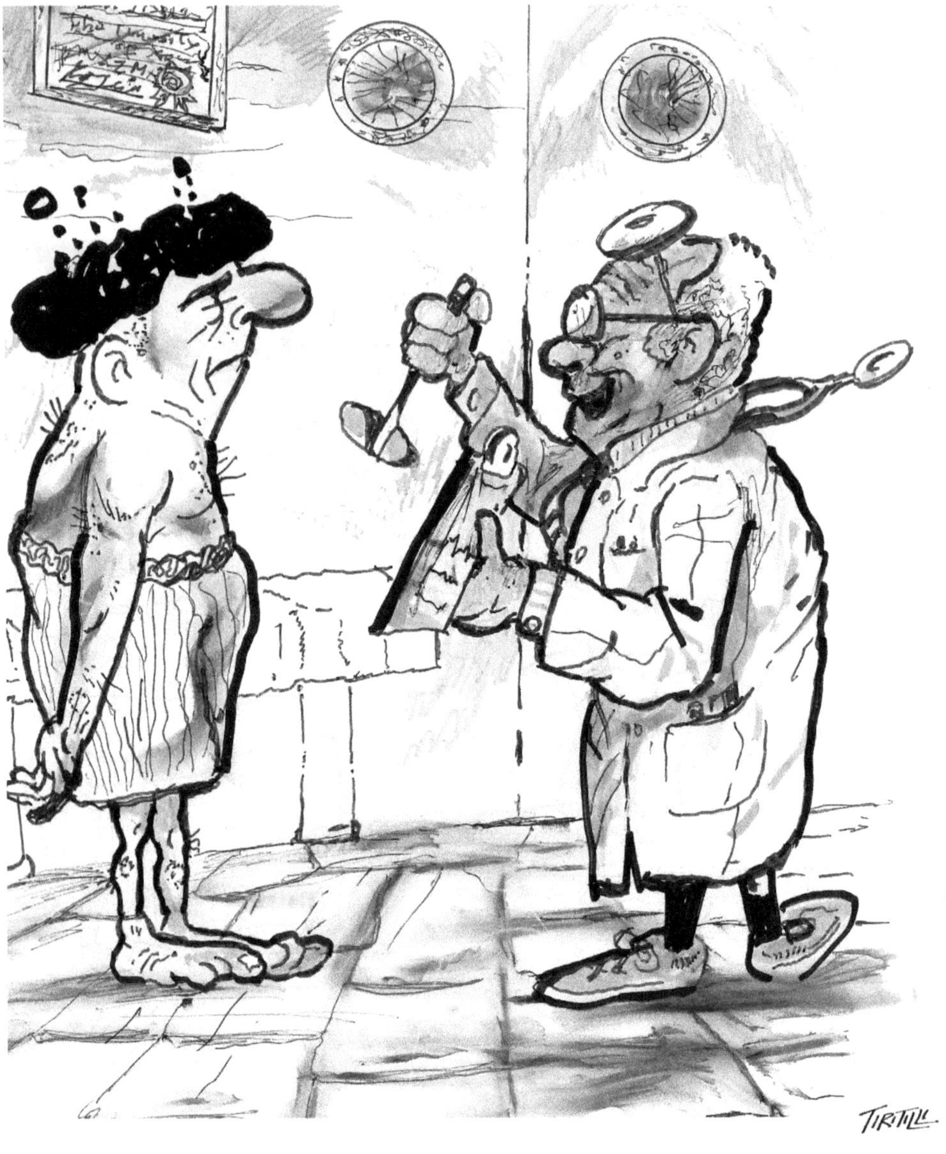

"I recommend walking to all my golf patients to give you an excellent cardio workout!"

"I got a golf scholarship, but
that didn't last too long!"

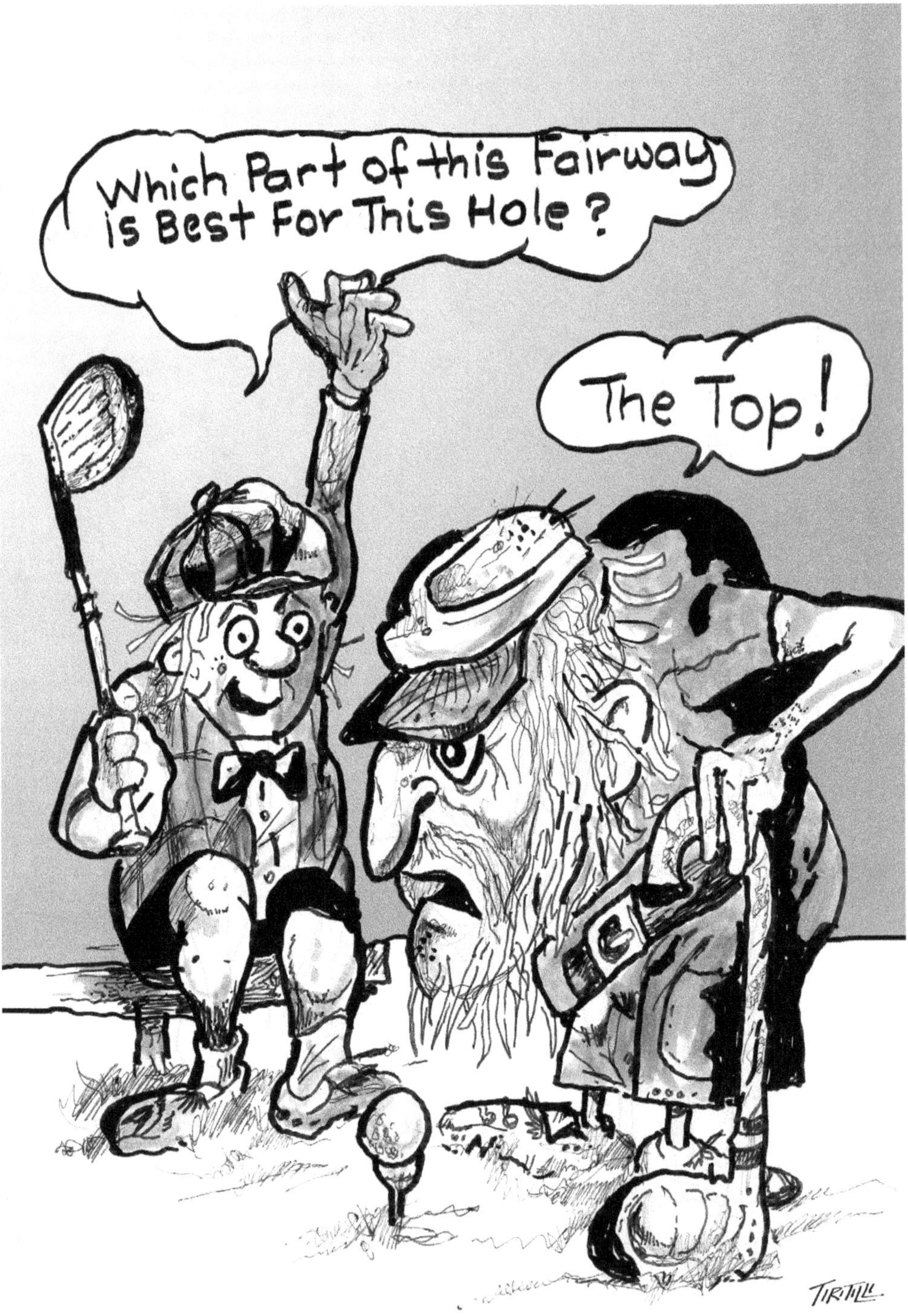
Which Part of this Fairway is Best For This Hole ?
The Top!
TIRITILLI

"Even TIGER can't
straighten out his slice!"

"You Bozo! Stop clowning around.
You're missing the *HOLE* point!"

"Golf should be given up
at least *twice* a month!"

"Don't buy a putter until you've had a chance to throw it!"

**"Golfers who claim
they don't cheat... *lie*!"**

"The higher a golfer's handicap makes him more qualified as an instructor!"

"Everyone's favorite sport...
buying sports equipment and goods!"

"Golf's world attitude toward
sport drugs!"

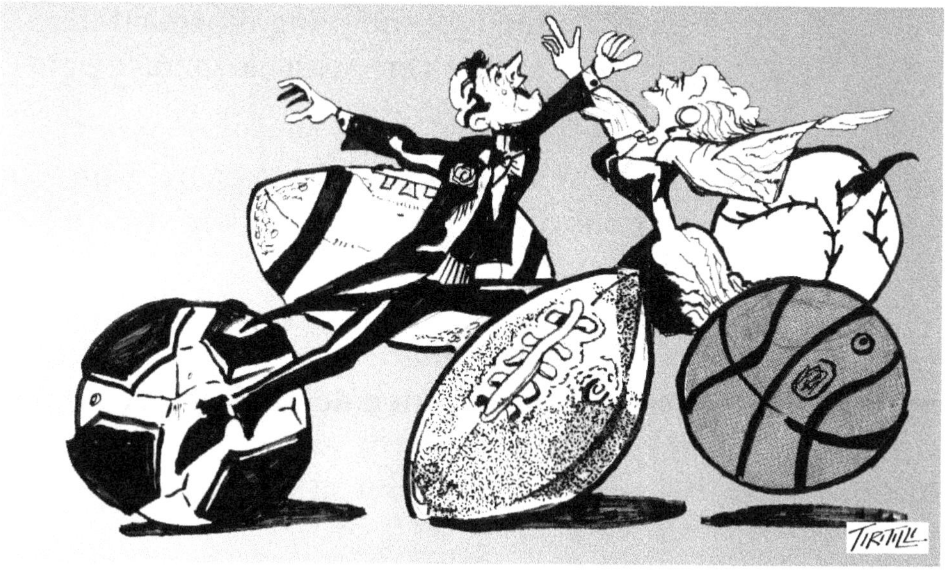
TIRITILLI

The Sports Ball

Robert A. Tiritilli

Award-winning cartoonist, Robert A. Tiritilli—a true sports aficionado—is passionate about all sports and loves to make fun of the pastime and all those who play it. He has drawn 1,000's of different sports cartoons and creates his outlandish style of sports cartooning by combining representative portraiture with cartoonish lightheartedness.

He uses a unique sense of silliness to strike a chord with anyone who plays or enjoys sports, whether they are athletes or couch potatoes.

He finds more ways to blend humorous cartoons with crafty captions. This cartoonist plays with a deck of cards containing every shade of sports humor—wit, satire, jesting, and clowning.

Laugh until your sides hurt with his collections of hilarious sports cartoons! Tiritilli has put the "F" back into the word "FUN." Sports has more words, terms, and phrases that lend themselves to humorous reinterpretation based on their literal meaning.

The fun of these cartoons at its best is when it shifts the meaning of a sports phrase into another one. But in some cases, the pictures take the obvious joke and make it better with a hilarious execution.

Robert A. Tiritilli

Robert A. Tiritilli is an artist who works in several mediums.
His favorite is the traditional pen & ink technique, which he
has produced thousands of detailed artworks. Recently,
he has created several works of graphic fine art in the
labor-intensive and time-consuming medium of scratchboarding.
Scratchboarding is a drawing technique whereby you scratch
or carve a design on the surface of a black board, revealing white
underneath. It has the opposite effect of drawing with black ink
on white paper. Since it is a reverse drawing method,
it requires learning special techniques to master it,
which Tiritilli did.

www.ingramcontent.com/pod-product-compliance
Lightning Source LLC
Chambersburg PA
CBHW061736020426

42331CB00006B/1263